SOUND HEALING FOR BEGINNERS

Sonic Medicine for the Body, Chakra Rituals, and What They Didn't Tell You About Vibrational Energy

ASCENDING VIBRATIONS

Ascending Vibrations

CONTENTS

BONUS GUIDED MEDITATION

Wouldn't it be nice to have even more motivation, inspiration, and courage on your spiritual path? As a sincere "Thank you" from the bottom of my heart, you can claim your downloadable 10 minute Energy Healing guided meditation Mp3 below.

Do you want to release toxicity within & realign with your true energy?

- STAND FIRM, say no, & set boundaries by owning your unique power & energy
- Become a magnet for other high vibrational energies
- Protect yourself from those in your life who have energy imbalances & are lowering your vibration

Go to this link to Get Your Free 10 minute Energy Healing Guided Meditation Mp3:

bit.ly/energyhealingfree

INTRODUCTION

You are energy and energy only. Your energy is arranged in a particular form that makes you the human being you are. Your particles are always moving within their assigned form, always alive with possibility, and vibrating at a frequency that keeps them healthy and in the right form.

This movement is known by many different names, including qi, prana, and spirit.

Anything that upsets the frequency brings about the 'wrong' movement for a body, organ, or system. We experience that as discomfort and disease. Our particles are not at ease anymore and the music their movements make together is dissonant instead of harmonious.

Introducing the right sound at the right vibrational frequency to bring your particles back to the frequency they want and should be in, is called sound healing.

And that is the subject matter of this book in a nutshell.

Get ready to be amazed and inspired by the power within your body and its connection to the universe. Your journey to become the best version of yourself that you can be starts here.

Through the practical and easy exercises in this ebook, you can reclaim the ancient wisdom about healing and health. Supercharge your understanding by reading and applying the knowledge.

Do the numerous practical sound and toning exercises, with and without instruments and tools.

Challenge yourself to learn overtone singing through the thorough explanations provided and give yourself the gift of harmonics, taking your healing practice to the next level.

Feel the calming and restoring benefits instantly when you do the step-by-step meditations provided in a later chapter while listening to a soundtrack on a specific frequency, binaural beats, or a natural soundscape through your earphones.

This is a hands-on (or should we say note-on) handbook to rediscover the power of sound as the ancient civilizations knew and used it, to the benefit of themselves and the whole planet. We can take back our power by harnessing sound the way it was intended to be used. We can heal the earth before it's too late.

Keep reading to enter a hugely exciting new chapter in your life, with sound and music in their rightful places as your partners in a healthy and optimal life.

UNDERSTANDING SOUND CAN ALTER YOUR EXISTENCE PROFOUNDLY

The right frequency is life.

The **Lost Chord** (Music composed in 1877 by Arthur Sullivan, set to a poem by Adelaide Anne Procter) (Lin, n.d.).

> *"Seated one day at the organ*
> *I was weary and ill at ease.*
> *And my fingers wandered idly*
> *Over the noisy keys.*
> *I know not what I was playing*
> *Or what I was dreaming then;*
> *But I struck one chord of music*
> *Like the sound of a great Amen!*
> *Like the sound of a great Amen.*
> *It flooded the crimson twilight*
> *Like the close of an angel's psalm*
> *And it lay on my fevered spirit*
> *With a touch of infinite calm.*
> *It quieted pain and sorrow*
> *Like love overcoming strife;*

It seemed the harmonious echo
From our discordant life.
It linked all perplexéd meanings
Into one perfect peace
And trembled away into silence
As if it were loth to cease.
I have sought, but I seek it vainly
That one lost chord divine
Which came from the soul of the organ
And entered into mine.
It may be that death's bright angel
Will speak in that chord again.
It may be that only in Heav'n
I shall hear that grand Amen."

This poem may be old but the fundamental truth about sound being a primal force in the universe remains true. Understanding sound and its role in life fully can make a profound difference to the rest of your existence, as well as to the health of our universe.

Sound has both scientific and emotional, metaphysical, and therapeutic uses in our lives. Our modern lifestyles have mostly pushed the scientific side to the foreground while neglecting the rest, often because they cannot produce economic and technological progress in our commercially oriented way of thinking.

Many of us are paying a steep price for doing that. Lifestyle diseases such as diabetes and cardiovascular problems, and mental problems such as depression, are at an all-time high worldwide. Stress has become the number one chronic problem and we have not even comprehended fully how much damage that does to our bodies and minds.

According to a recent report by the World Health Organization on non-communicable diseases, lifestyle diseases account for 71% of all global deaths each year. More than 15 million people die between the ages of 30 and 69 when they still should have had a productive life ahead of them. Cardiovascular diseases cause the most deaths, followed by various forms of cancer, respiratory diseases, and diabetes. Obesity due to chronic stress and harmful lifestyle habits contribute significantly to all these numbers (WHO, 2021).

Using sound to heal and comfort is one of the oldest forms of healing. It is believed to have originated in ancient Greece, where healers tried to cure mental illness with music.

Music is used to stimulate mental and physical processes, and speed up recovery from illnesses, throughout the world. It is used to increase productivity in the workplace, boost the morale of military troops, and ward off evil spirits in some cultures (Santos-Longhurst, 2020).

A session of sound, whether experienced in a group or individually, can help you unwind tense muscles and stop anxious thoughts from spinning out of control through your head.

The right vibrations will bring harmony back into your body and mind, clearing any blockages that prevent an optimum state of health and happiness. It can bring about deep healing from traumas and open up energy pathways and the chakras once more.

Sound healing can help to lower blood pressure, make chronic pain more bearable, and aid in deep sleep.

WHAT IS SOUND?

To answer this question, we would have to determine what the nature and influence of vibrations are, first.

Have you ever been in your house when a big truck roared past and you heard a faint, rattling hum in the window panes? Even more than that, can you remember experiencing a vibration in your very bones, corresponding to the deep rumble of the vehicle's engine?

That is sound and vibration at work.

According to the scientific definition, sound is a pressure wave that is caused by a vibrating object. The vibration sets particles of air in motion and our ears pick up the pressure wave (University of Toronto Computer Science, 2004).

In our ears, the vibration caused by the pressure wave is turned into electrical signals that our brains pick up through the auditory nerve and interpret (National Institute on Deafness and Other Communication Disorders, Maryland, 2015).

The particles transporting the energy of the wave, which is usually air, move parallel to the pressure wave. Sound is therefore called a longitudinal wave.

The height and depth to which the particles oscillate before coming back to the middle line are called the amplitude of a sound. The number of complete back-and-forth movements of a particle in a second is measured in Hertz (Hz) and called the frequency of the sound. The faster the movement is, which results in a higher frequency, the higher-pitched the sound is. The speed at which the sound wave travels is called the wavelength (University of Toronto Computer Science, 2004).

HOW DO WE HEAR?

Our basic hearing mechanisms are our eardrums and a couple of tiny bones.

Sound waves enter our ears through the ear canal that leads to the eardrum. The eardrum is a thin, cone-shaped tissue membrane that is covered with skin on the outside and mucus on the inside of the ear. The membrane vibrates from the sound waves.

The vibrations travel to three small bones in the middle ear called the malleus, incus, and stapes. This amplifies the sound before it is passed on to the cochlea, which is a snail-shaped, fluid-filled structure in the inner ear.

The cochlea is divided into an upper and lower part by a partition called the basilar membrane, which is covered with sensory cells shaped like hairs.

The sound waves cause the fluid in the cochlea to ripple and it creates a wave on top of the basilar membrane. The hair cells and the micro projections on top of them called stereocilia bump against the structure above them. As they bend during the bumping movement, small channels open up. Chemicals enter the channels, sending electrical signals to the brain through the auditory nerve.

The brain interprets the signals and turns them into sounds we can understand (National Institute on Deafness and Other Communication Disorders, Maryland, 2015).

HOW DO SOUNDS INFLUENCE US?

You might ask how sound can affect our emotional and physical wellbeing.

Besides obvious things such as acting as a warning in dangerous situations, sound can have a profound effect. It cannot be turned off like unwanted sights can be shut out by closing the eyes.

Just as the sound entering our awareness is a vibration on a certain frequency, our organs vibrate on their own specific frequencies. The frequency of an incoming sound may amplify our frequencies, or oppose them.

In a study conducted on the relationship between our DNA and sound, scientists found that the three-dimensional scalar grid of non-coding substance that our DNA incorporates besides the coding part contains data that relates to electrical impulses created by oral, as well as written language. The patterns of a language translate into mathematical codes used for communication in the wholeness of our consciousness. They describe it as a blueprint with operational instructions for our spirit-mind-body matrix. That is profound—communicated sound instructs our consciousness through a holographic library of data! This occurs in the part of our DNA that is usually ignored by scientists as 'junk-DNA' (Rivera-Dugenio, 2019).

It is, therefore, safe to say that sound is a carrier of consciousness with far more power in our existence than it looks. It will not be an overstatement to say we can make or break our world with sound.

It is our choice what we will do with the sounds we spend our time with and what their quality will be. Through sound healing techniques, we can benefit not only our physical bodies but access our spiritual and mental bodies to bring us back to the state of equilibrium and wellness we were intended to be in.

This state of wellness extends to our environment and the rest of the cosmos. Remember the psychological concept known as the butterfly effect? According to the postulated theory, the mere sound of a butterfly's wings in one part of the world can cause a violent storm in another part of the world.

That is not a far-fetched idea anymore. We do not have to see something to feel its effect upon our consciousness, as was demonstrated in a scientific experiment where unseen sounds brought visual signals into participants' awareness. The strength of the visual perception was independent of the volume of the sound flash (Aller et al., 2015).

THE BUILDING BLOCKS OF SOUND HEALING

There are a couple of mainstays that have to be explained when talking about sound healing. One of the most important of these is resonance.

Resonance

Every object in the universe has a natural frequency at which it vibrates. If an external force, vibrating at a different frequency, touches the object, the contact will force the object to find its natural frequency and start vibrating at it. That, in a nutshell, is how resonance works (The Physics Classroom, n.d.).

The external force does not necessarily have to be a physical object. It can be another sound, such as a note in a song, that sets the frequency of your body and its organs off to vibrate on their specific natural, healing frequencies. An example of this is when a note is sung in close proximity to a musical instrument such as a violin, and the string corresponding with that pitch starts sounding.

Sound healers believe organs that do not vibrate at the frequencies they are supposed to cause illness and a feeling of unease, also known in the world of natural healing as dis-ease (Encyclopedia.com, 2014).

Intent

According to experts in the field of sound healing, the right frequency alone is not enough to facilitate healing. The sound healer has to hold the intention of healing a person and/or organ in his heart and mind too (Goldman, 2009a).

This will be discussed in greater detail later in the ebook.

TYPES AND INSTRUMENTS OF SOUND THERAPY

A sound healing session can take several different forms, using a variety of instruments besides conventional music, to effect healing and de-stressing through sound. Each type has benefits for specific scenarios.

Tuning Forks

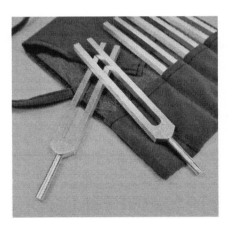

A set of tuning forks.

A tuning fork that is calibrated for a specific frequency can be touched to a part of the body that functions on that frequency, to balance and heal organs. The vibrations can open up blocked energy channels and release tension stored in the muscles.

It can also help to relieve pain.

Gongs

A set of gongs, with singing bowls in the foreground.

Gongs have been an integral part of sound healing since about 4,000 years ago (Bhaumik, 2019). The deep, rich sounds produced when a gong is hit produce strong vibrations that can put the brain into a meditation pattern within a minute.

Today, it is often used for gong baths.

Singing Bowls

Metal singing bowls.

Singing bowls were first used in Tibetan culture as early as the 12th century (Bhaumik, 2019).

They are usually made of metal and come in several sizes, each producing different vibrations that work on the mind and body.

The bowls can be placed onto the body so the water in the body cells can convey the vibrations directly to the organ that is targeted.

Wind Chimes

More than just a pretty window decoration, wind chimes date back many years to the Indian and Chinese civilizations.

They help to center and ground the mind and promote relaxation.

Crystals

Crystal singing bowls.

Singing bowls can also be made of crystals. The frequency that is released when a soft mallet is run around the edge of the bowl depends on the type of crystal the bowl is made of, as well as the size of the bowl.

The vibrations of the bowls can be enhanced when rock crystals are placed nearby.

Rock quartz crystals.

Didgeridoos

A modern street musician playing a large didgeridoo.

The Australian didgeridoo is a type of flute created from bamboo or wood. It originated about 1,500 years ago to be used in spiritual ceremonies.

It is believed to be highly effective in unblocking stagnant energy.

Djembes

A traditional djembe.

A djembe is a Western African drum made of wood and covered with goat hide and rope. It is commonly used to start and enhance trance states, as well as give a boost to meditation.

It is often used in drumming circles to alleviate stress.

Kalimbas

Kalimbas range from fairly sophisticated to very basic.

Another instrument of African origin, the kalimba is also sometimes called a thumb piano. It consists of a small wooden platform with metal keys mounted on it.

It is used for its calming effect.

Hammered Dulcimer

A hammered dulcimer.

A hammered dulcimer is a string instrument reminiscent of a zither that originated in medieval Europe. It has strings stretched over a wooden frame acting as a sound box, with two strings for every note. The strings are hit with light hammers to produce the sound rather than plucked.

It is commonly used to calm the mind and bring peace to upset emotions. It is a great meditation aid.

Monochords

Several monochords sharing a single sound box to demonstrate harmonic intervals.

A monochord is a one-stringed instrument that is said to have been invented by the Greek philosopher and mathematician Pythagoras.

The vibrations of the string are thought to bring renewed energy to the body and mind.

Native American Flutes

A traditional musician holding a native American flute.

The soothing sound emitted by these flutes is well-known and loved in sound healing. It is used to reduce stress and anxiety.

The usage of the flute is also known as Ojibwe music, after the Ojibwe or Chippewa tribe that was one of the most powerful tribes of North America.

Rain Sticks

A rain stick.

The origins of these shakers lie in the Aztec culture. They used dried, hollow cactus that they filled with seeds or small stones. When shaken, the sticks make a sound resembling rain.

They are used to promote relaxation and decrease anxiety.

Hanghang

Hanghang can vary from small to large.

A hang handpan percussion instrument (the plural being 'hanghang') is a Swedish creation dating only a couple of years back.

It is somewhat similar to a singing bowl and produces deeply melodic sounds that are great for relaxing, while at the same time boosting focus and concentration for meditating.

Solfeggio Frequencies

Listening to a solfeggio frequency through earphones can minimize distractions.

The solfeggio frequencies are six tones that vibrate with specific organs and body parts. The tones are named according to the sol-fa designation, which consists of Ut-Re-Mi-Fa-Sol-La.

It is believed these six tones have been used since ancient times to promote healing and balance. See a more in-depth discussion of solfeggio tones later in the book.

Binaural Beats

This mode of sound healing is also known as brain entrainment. It uses pulsing, subtle beats that encourage the human brain to align to their frequencies and enter a specific state. The beats are sometimes set to music.

The concept will be discussed fully in a later chapter.

Rhythm and Voice

Using music as a healing tool will be discussed in greater detail in a later chapter. It can involve creating music, listening to it, singing, or moving to the beat.

Meditation

Meditation, with or without chanting a mantra, is one of the first to come to mind when thinking about sound healing. A mantra helps prevent your mind from drifting, ensuring you get the full benefit of meditation.

The sounds produced by the voice when chanting a mantra during meditation create vibrations in the body, which can aid healing.

The same goes for a humming meditation, where the vibrations of the hum originate within the body and stimulate the vagus nerve for various benefits.

See a later chapter for a more in-depth discussion of meditation and its benefits.

Harmony

The harmonies that are created when different notes blend, combine vibrations to form a powerful healing force. Administering healing through harmony requires a solid knowledge of the effects of various harmonies on the body and mind.

Harmonic relationships will be thoroughly discussed later in the book.

Humming

The strong vibrations of humming pervade the whole body. Coupled with effective deep breathing, humming exercises create powerful healing sessions.

Nature Soundscapes

It is no coincidence that certain sounds of nature are soothing or inspiring. The frequencies of sounds such as ocean waves or water running over pebbles can influence us in powerful ways.

THE IMPORTANCE OF HOMEOSTASIS

In the end, all these methods of healing aim to bring the mental, physical, and emotional body back into homeostasis. This state of equilibrium allows optimal functioning, without any component being in discomfort or disease because it is out of balance with the rest.

Although only the physical body can be seen by others, it does not exist in isolation from the mental and emotional (or energy) bodies—all are interdependent.

THE FORGOTTEN SUPERPOWER:
LISTENING

Hearing is automatic but listening is not.

Without listening, there can be no sound healing. It is a prerequisite for healing to take place. The sounds and their vibrations have to become part of your body to reap the full benefit of the treatment.

There are different ways in which we listen, and not all of them involve the ears. There is a big difference between simply hearing and listening. When you listen, you move beyond the physical process of using your auditory organs to give meaning to the things you hear.

Listening is also just as much about your inner voice, as it is about what other people say and do.

OUTER LISTENING

To hear with the ears is an automatic activity that does not require any skills. Our ears are always on, therefore our brains have to apply filters to determine which sounds register in our consciousness.

This filtering process, through which we make sense of the sounds our ears hear from outside our physical bodies, is called outer listening.

It is always colored by our personal experiences and preferences and can be passive or active.

INNER LISTENING

In contrast to listening to sounds from outside, inner listening pertains to the voice inside our heads. This voice is very much influenced by our feelings, preferences, and past experiences.

An important and powerful point to realize regarding the inner voice is that it is not who we are. It is our hurts, embarrassments, and past disappointments (mostly) speaking and we are the ones listening.

Being the listener means we can discard any suggestions or information we do not consider helpful or accurate. That brings enormous personal power and peace.

CREATED LISTENING

Our perceptions of who a person is or what he/she represents, color our way of listening to that person. It is also a set of filters that we apply, sometimes without being aware of doing it.

It can cause misunderstandings because our preconceived ideas of what a person is saying, might not be what the person really is trying to communicate.

DEEP LISTENING

When you listen to learn with an open and receptive mind, whether from your inner voice or someone else, it is known as deep listening. The purpose of the listening must be to understand, even if agreement cannot be reached (Bakken Center for Spirituality and Healing, 2015).

Deep listening also involves asking powerful questions. A powerful question draws the person into the real meaning of the conversation and inspires them to reflect on it.

To practice this mode of listening, the listener has to empty his mind and open up to receive the information the other person has not shared yet in words.

In sound healing, this principle applies to one's ability to hear your own inner voice and to allow it to say the things your core being knows but has not spoken about yet.

- Become aware of the present moment first. Feel your body, clothes, and environment without thinking any words. Try to become really quiet within yourself. Experience your center of gravity and ground yourself.
- Now, become aware of and acknowledge anything that could be interfering with your quietness. Accept that you have feelings, judgments, fears, and sensations that move in your mind. These things are the triggers that can stop you from deeply listening to yourself and allowing sound to heal you.
- Once you have identified your triggers, try to understand where they come from, without judging or criticizing yourself. Then will you be able to move on to a deeper understanding of yourself.

MINDFUL AND CONSCIOUS LISTENING

If we silence all the inner voices, outer noises, and become aware of our personal filters, we can listen with an open mind to another person or happening. That is being fully conscious of the moment.

The increasingly noisy environment in which most of us find ourselves constantly is stumping our ability to listen with a conscious and active attitude. Our brains get overwhelmed by a bombardment of stimuli and it is sometimes easier to simply shut down. By doing so, we enter into a prison of our own making, where we deny ourselves the rich life of healing and soothing sounds.

What is Mindfulness?

Many people equate mindfulness with meditation but meditating is only one way of practicing mindfulness. Mindfulness practice in conjunction with sound healing can be used for dramatic results.

Mindfulness can be described as being fully aware of everything inside and outside you, without passing judgments on anything. It means simply noticing them with no interruptions.

To do that, the inner voice has to be silenced or bypassed, at least. It might seem difficult to do in the beginning but it becomes easy when a couple of simple things are kept in mind.

- The first point, being present in the first place, seems self-explanatory but it can seem tricky if you're not used to it yet. It helps to simplify all your surroundings and remove distractions as far as possible. Switch off the television and cell phone and put the computer away. Put a "do not disturb" sign on the door. Make sure anything on your desk that could distract your attention is also tidied up or put away in a drawer. Straighten your furniture and decor if you tend to get distracted by an untidy environment.
- Sit quietly for a minute or two before starting a listening experience, whether it is a meeting with another person or a healing session. Prepare yourself mentally for what you are about to experience. Visualize emptying your head of all the thoughts that will interfere with your full immersion in the material you will be listening to.
- Relax with a breathing exercise and muscle stress release. Focusing on your breathing to the exclusion of everything else is a form of meditation that can help muscles release the tension stored deep inside.

When you start paying attention to your breathing, chances are that you will find your breath is shallow. Inhalations typically don't go deeper than the upper chest and never reach the abdomen. That limits the amount of oxygen that reaches the body.

In contrast, diaphragmatic or belly breathing pulls the lungs downward and opens them up to receive much more oxygen. This reduces stress and has beneficial effects on blood pressure and heart rate.

When the breathing has deepened, you can combine it with contracting groups of muscles, one after the other, before releasing the tension. Move through the whole body and pay special attention to any muscles that store tension, such as the shoulders, neck, and abdomen.

- Centering is another excellent way to get into and remain in the present. While breathing deeply, become aware of your physical center of gravity. It is usually just below the waistline.

Focus all your attention on your center while breathing deeply at least another five times more. Be aware that you are in balance and have control.

Visualize all the negative energy collected in your body, concentrated in your center where you control it. Move the ball of negative energy up towards your eyes and then push it out and away from you. That leaves you calm, grounded, and happily present.

- Lastly, it is important to become aware of the cues, or triggers, that launch the filters that color your listening. Once you can see and feel them happening, you can sidestep them and remain open and mindfully listening.

NADA YOGA

The Vedic tradition has something that can be described as sound yoga. It is called nada yoga.

The word 'nada' refers to the vibration of sound. In this form of yoga, sound is used not only to heal and balance body and mind but also to open the path to true spiritual awakening.

In nada yoga, a distinction is made between internal and external sounds.

External sounds, or ahata in Sanskrit, are heard through the ears. It can be practiced by something as simple as listening to calming non-vocal music and picking out the individual notes to focus on.

Nature also has sounds like birdsong, rain, or the wind rustling in the leaves. Chanting a mantra also represents ahata.

The point is to listen to external sounds in such a way that it opens up the door for you to travel inward, into yourself.

Internal sounds are called anahata in Sanskrit. They are perceived through the anahata, or heart, chakra.

These sounds are the sacred inner music that is unique to each individual. When the breath is regulated and the sight is turned inward, these sounds can be perceived to balance the energy bodies and re-establish a connection with your true and divine self.

Some people can hear the cosmos itself hum after a time of rigorous practice.

MORE EXERCISES IN MINDFULNESS

To make the most of sound healing, you have to be able to listen effectively. In our modern, noisy world it does not come automatically anymore.

Silence

A meaningful silence is more than a mere absence of sounds. It has a voice of its own because vibrations never cease. It can be as therapeutic as music or voice.

Many people have become afraid of silence because it is something strange in a world that never sleeps. In the task-centered Western world, being silent is often construed as unproductiveness or laziness.

Eastern philosophies and most religions around the world make much of quiet contemplation, though. It brings an opportunity to reflect on what is really going on around and inside us, something that scares some people away. To someone who is used to being on the move constantly, producing results, being quiet can feel like a sort of death, which is scary for most of us.

There is, however, great healing in connecting with the self and hearing the inner voice again. In the quiet times, the true vibrations of our being can make themselves heard.

Sound expert Julian Treasure calls the periodic immersion in total silence 'recalibration' of our ears. It brings back awareness of subtle sounds while sensitizing us again to sounds that are loud enough to potentially damage our hearing (Treasure, 2017).

Try to experience silence for at least three minutes every day. It can be challenging to find a quiet spot but choose somewhere that has as few sounds as possible. It can work well just after waking up or just before dozing off at night.

When you meditate, try to do it in silence, focusing on your breathing alone. While music and guided meditations can be beneficial, especially in the beginning, having music and the voice of a guide can remove stillness as you progress.

Isolate Sounds

Another effective way to practice conscious listening is to try and isolate individual sounds when you are in a noisy environment such as a mall.

Try to identify the different elements that make up the auditory 'soup' that is known as mall mush. Zooming the focus like a spotlight forces the brain to concentrate on the immediate environment, helping to create a habit of being present and mindful.

Noticing The Raisin

For this exercise, any other kind of food with an interesting texture will also work.

Take the raisin in your hand and look at it really closely. Notice the feel of it against your skin, as well as the weight. Look at the color and whether it is shiny or not.

Smell the raisin and savor any aroma you pick up.

Gently squeeze the fruit and notice how it changes shape.

Don't judge anything you notice during this exercise, just note it and let it pass.

This is a conscious listening practice that can supercharge your sound healing practices over time.

THE BODY SCAN

Sit comfortably in a chair with your feet on the ground or lie down on your back, feet slightly apart. Close your eyes and try to stay as still as possible for the whole duration of the exercise.

Quiet your mind and start paying attention to all the sections of your body, starting at the top and moving down to your feet.

Note to yourself which parts feel relaxed, tight, warm, cool, tired, or sore. Become aware of how the bed/chair and your clothes feel against each body part. Notice your breathing.

Take your time to become fully present to every sensation in and against your body. This is equivalent to entering into a mindful conversation with your body, with you as the compassionate listener.

Once you have finished the scan, open your eyes when you feel ready and sit up again.

A Mind Scan

The same principle as in the exercise above can be applied to your thoughts and feelings. This is a great way to learn to keep a quiet, open mind, flowing like water.

Take five minutes in which you imagine your feelings and thoughts as fish gliding through the water—you see them, but you don't try to catch them or pin them down for dissection. You just note their existence.

You also acknowledge the sensations these thoughts and feelings create in you, without trying to evaluate or label them.

Mindful Watching

Position yourself near a window where there is some scenery outside to observe. It can be nature or a busy city sidewalk, wherever you find yourself.

Watch the scene with your mind as well as your eyes, without cognitively naming any objects. Notice, for instance, the texture of the leaves on the tree and the way they move in the breeze without thinking 'tree' to yourself. Just watch.

Don't evaluate or pass judgment on anything.

Notice if you get distracted and gently leave those thoughts to return to watching.

Let Your Senses Do the Talking

This is an easy and fun exercise to do with children especially but adults benefit from it greatly, too.

Make a mental list of five things you can see, four things you can touch and feel, three things you can hear, two things you can smell, and one thing you can taste.

The aforementioned conscious listening practices in conjunction with sound healing makes for a potent recipe indeed.

PRIMORDIAL SOUND

The teachings about the primordial or primeval and basic sound of the universe originated centuries ago in the Vedic system of wisdom from India.

The contemporary philosopher Deepak Chopra revived the tradition and developed meditations using a person's personal primordial sound at the time of his/her birth, as the mantra. The personal mantra is calculated according to Vedic mathematics and astrology to determine which sound the universe made at the time of the individual's birth.

Incorporating the sound in the person's meditation mantra brings him/her back into contact with their innate wisdom and peaceful silence, what primordial meditation expert Julie Hunt calls "the space of infinite possibility between thoughts" (Hunt, 2020).

This is accomplished through chanting the mantra ohm (auhm) + personalized sound + m + namah. In between, four questions are asked of the self, in silence: Who am I, what do I want, what is my purpose, and what am I grateful for?

At the end of the meditation, four core intentions are left in the silence and sent into the universe. These are for having a joyful, energetic body, a compassionate and loving heart, an alert and reflective mind, and a lightness of being (Hunt, 2020).

Benefits of Primordial Meditation

Primordial sounds are considered to be the most basic sounds of nature and, as such, are believed to help us disconnect from everyday busyness. The basic vibrations that make up the universe can align our own vibrations again with our true purpose and a deep sense of peace. It allows us to be fully aware without any intellectual questioning or evaluations, and experience the innate stillness that is within all of us.

Meditation has been shown by several studies to have a beneficial effect on stress and emotion-related disorders (Goyal et al., 2014).

In another study, the participants also recorded higher subjective energy levels and an improvement in handling conflict (Walsh et al., 2019).

SOUND HEALING FOR TINNITUS

When the organs we use to hear the healing sounds develop problems, it affects much more than hearing. Tinnitus, which causes a person to hear sounds such as ringing, hissing, buzzing, or whistling that don't exist, affects millions of people worldwide. Statistics from the American Tinnitus Association show that almost 20 million Americans alone suffer from the condition chronically (Clason, 2019).

Currently, there is no treatment for the condition yet, but sound therapy is recognized as a successful treatment. It works through retraining the brain to stop noticing the sound, thereby eliminating the disturbance.

Audiologists use sounds we perceive as neutral, such as waves on the shore or falling rain. The sound is played continuously throughout the day and gradually the brain starts to equate the tinnitus sound with the neutral sound. The offending sound is, in effect, simply 'relegated' to the subconscious. The important point to keep in mind is that the volume of the background sound should not be loud enough to drown out the tinnitus sound. It should co-exist with the tinnitus for the training to take place (Clason, 2019).

Recent scientific studies have shown this type of treatment to be effective for a broad range of tinnitus sufferers. It is an excellent example of how profoundly sound can affect our lives (Wang et al., 2020).

❧ 3 ❧
CREATING MAGIC WITH VOCAL
TONING

The experiments performed by Swiss medical doctor Hans Jenny in the 1960s to show how sound can change formless matter into intricate patterns are well-known. Jenny put powders, liquids, and pastes on steel plates and vibrated the plates on pure frequencies generated by a crystal oscillator. The photographs he took of the structured patterns that the substances formed can be found in the two volumes he wrote about the field in physics he called cymatics (Goldman & Sims, 2016).

You don't need plates and crystal oscillators to create with sound, though. Your voice is all you need.

Are you ready to experience the power of the musical instrument you were born with?

HOW DOES VOCAL TONING WORK?

Going back to the basic premise of sound healing, which is that every cell in the human body vibrates at its specific frequency and that the body functions as a harmonious unit when all the cells are at the correct frequency, it follows that the voice can correct imbalances easier than external instruments.

Goldman and Sims make the observation in their book *Sound*

Healing for Beginners (2016) that not all the recordings that claim to be of specific frequencies are, in fact, on the same frequency. Even with the variety, people using the recordings report success. That creates the question of whether we all are vibrating at individual frequencies. If the answer to that is yes, it makes an even stronger case for the use of the voice in healing. There is no definitive conclusion about the question yet.

THE FOUNDATION

It has to be understood clearly that using the voice as a healing instrument is not about singing. It can be speaking, humming, chanting, or simple sounds like breathing. Don't let the vocal part put you off from trying this amazing technique if you have any doubts about your singing ability.

One similarity vocal toning does have with singing is that it relies on conscious breathing. Breathing can change heart rate and brain states, which can alter consciousness itself (Goldman & Sims, 2016).

Every vocal toning session should start with attention to abdominal breathing, a technique that has been discussed in a previous chapter.

In addition to breathing in and releasing the breath immediately, the breath can also be held in for a couple of seconds before releasing it slowly.

Another excellent breathing exercise is the three-point-focused approach. Start the inhalation by focusing on the abdomen. While you feel it filling with air, shift to your ribs and fill that region with air. Next, direct your focus to your lungs. When you feel your lungs are about 90 percent filled with air, expand your awareness to the base of your throat and your collarbone and allow everything to expand—you should experience a pleasant sensation of relaxed openness at the base of the throat. Hold the breath for a second or two, savoring the feeling of being completely filled with air. Then gradually exhale by relaxing the diaphragm.

Exhaling completely but in a controlled way is just as important as inhaling fully. Rather than forcing the air out in one go, try to let it out to a count of four. A controlled exhalation sustains vocal work. As you get more comfortable with the technique, you can extend the exhalation count to eight or even more. The key is to remain comfortable with how you are doing it.

ADDING SOUND

With the foundation of breathing under your belt, so to speak, it is time to add the first sound to the inhalations and exhalations.

Add any gentle sound that feels natural to you. A s-s-sound on inhaling and an ahh-sound on exhaling work for most people. Reverse the sounds after a couple of breaths and notice any subtle differences in energy you might feel. Even the smallest change in sound can have a big influence on energy fields and our experience of them.

The Importance of Silence

Incorporating a short period of quiet contemplation after each vocal exercise is just as important as the sound itself. That gives you the chance to assimilate the shift that has just taken place and move it from your subconscious to your conscious experience, to reap the full benefits.

Exercise 1: Humming

The humming sound is directed inwards and so it is easier for the inexperienced in sound work to focus on it. Choose any pitch that feels comfortable to you, in the middle of your vocal range. Always remember, vocal toning is not about performance, although regular vocal work can result in unexpected improvements to your singing and speaking voice.

Make sure your facial muscles and your tongue are relaxed when your mouth is closed. If you detect any tension, yawn and sigh a couple of times to loosen them up.

Make a hmmm-sound on your chosen pitch and sustain it for as long as is comfortable on one breath. Note where you feel the resonance. It could be a ticklish sensation in your nose and head sinuses, as well as the back of the throat and the upper chest.

Start another humming sound but imagine you are making an ng-sound (as in the word sing) with your mouth still closed. Note where you feel the resonance now.

For the next round, imagine you are humming on an oh-sound and again be aware of where the resonance shifts.

Now you can start playing with the pitch. Go up and down the musical scale as high and as low as you can go. As the shape of your vocal cords changes with the change in pitch, the resonance will shift throughout your body.

Exercise 2: Focused Humming

Taking humming a step further, focus on any area in your body such as the solar plexus or the base of the spine, before starting to hum.

Start producing the sound and see if you feel any reaction from the targeted body part. Change the pitch and see if the energy shifts from there, or reach that body part if the first sound has not elicited any reaction.

Try to move through your whole body with this exercise but keep the total session to five or ten minutes in the beginning, until you are used to it and can keep your concentration for longer periods.

To enhance the strength of the humming even more, you can cover your ears lightly with your hands while humming and try to make the softest sound you can. Notice that while the sound may be barely detectable for outsiders, the resonance inside your body might be amplified.

Exercise 3: Open Voice

A warm-up exercise that singers often use is the siren. It is not difficult to do and simply requires you to let go of your voice, like a child.

Start at the lowest pitch comfortable to you and, making any sound such as ah, glide your sound up to the highest pitch you can manage. It does not have to be loud and there should be no strain involved.

Then reverse the sound, moving from the highest pitch down to the lowest.

Keep to the counting pattern used in the breathing exercises, inhaling on a count of four and letting the sound out on a count of four or eight, whatever you can manage comfortably.

The Power of Laughter

Of all the natural sounds we produce, laughter is one of the most healing vibrations. It is not only an emotional release but also brings about powerful shifts in energy vibrations. There is also scientific evidence of the beneficial physical changes that laughter can bring about.

A study done by researchers at the University of Maryland School of Medicine in Baltimore in 2005 found that a daily dose of laughter causes the inner lining of blood vessels, called the endothelium, to dilate, which increases the blood flow to all body systems. Increased blood flow means higher oxygen levels, which protect the heart, brain, and other organs, and strengthen the immune system.

A group of 20 healthy, non-smoking male and female individuals were shown 15 minutes of a movie that stimulated laughter. Their baseline blood vessel dilation was measured before they started, and again after watching the scenes, and significant dilation was found.

Some hours later, the baseline measurements of the same group of volunteers were taken again. They were then shown a 15-minute segment of a movie that caused them mental agitation and stress. Their endothelium this time showed constriction, which is the first step toward hardening of the arteries and cardiovascular disease.

The endothelium also secretes chemicals that regulate blood flow and coagulation when injuries and infections are detected.

The leader of the study, Dr. Michael Miller, equated the benefits seen after the laughing session to the effects of aerobic exercise, but without the exertion and aches (University Of Maryland Medical Center, 2005).

Exercise 4: Laughing

Settle yourself where you won't have to worry about other people listening and thinking you've lost your mind. Start with a deep inhalation and breathe out with a sigh. Take another breath and expel it with a soft chuckle.

Continue breathing and chuckling gently to yourself. Notice if you're starting to smile and spontaneously moving from chuckling to real laughter—it might feel silly at first, but that is fine.

When you feel you have finished laughing, quiet down and take a few moments to reflect if you feel any different.

Repeat the exercise and exhale on tones that might differ from your natural laughing sound. Do ha, ho, and he. Notice where in your body the sounds resonated. 'Ho' is usually felt low, 'ha' more in the middle, and 'he' in the upper body and head.

You can also vary the pitch for each sound.

Finish with combining the sounds and moving the resonance up and down your body.

TONING SOUNDS FOR DIFFERENT PARTS OF THE BODY

Some sounds work specifically on particular parts of the body. That is in contrast to the vowel sounds, which are non-specific. Chanting a vowel sound and mentally directing it to the area you want to target will work just as well.

Here are a few examples of tones that work well for certain organs (Gabriel, 2015):

Mmmm	Sinus cavities
Mamm	Reproductive system
Wooo	Bladder and kidneys
Shhh	Small intestine and liver
Nnnn	Ears
Lemm	Nose
Maaa	Heart and surrounding muscles
Ssss	Large intestine and lungs
Paam	Stomach
Kaa-Gaa-Gha	Throat and larynx
Yaa-Yuu-Yii	Jaw and teeth
Haaa	Diaphragm muscle
Eemm	Eyes
Uu-Ah-Ee-Mm	Waking up and energizing
Mm-Ee-Ah-Uu	Relaxing, getting ready for bed

HEALING AND CLEARING THE CHAKRAS

Chakras are spinning energy centers situated at various spots through the body. There are seven of them and each one is thought to correlate to specific organs and nerve bundles. It is important to keep them in balance for optimum emotional and physical health (Stelter, 2016).

The First Chakra: The Root

Located at the base of the spine, it is associated with grounding and physical identity. The color is red.

Imbalances in this chakra can make a person feel emotionally unstable and experience feelings of insecurity about their ability to meet their basic needs. On the physical level, a root imbalance is associated with issues such as constipation, urinary tract infections, and arthritis (Stelter, 2016).

The Second Chakra: The Sacral

The sacral energy center is located just below the belly button and above the pubic bone. It is associated with the color orange, as well as sexual health, creativity, and the capacity to experience pleasure in general.

Problems with lower back pain, infertility, and impotency can result from a sacral imbalance. On the emotional side, self-image and our feelings of self-worth, particularly in terms of experiencing pleasure on all levels, can suffer if this chakra is not balanced (Stelter, 2016).

The Third Chakra: The Solar Plexus

It is located in the area of the stomach, in the upper abdomen, and the associated color is yellow. It rules confidence and the experience of personal power.

If the solar plexus chakra is misaligned, it can cause feelings of helplessness and a victim mentality. Physically speaking, ulcers, indigestion, and eating disorders can result (Stelter, 2016).

The Fourth Chakra: The Heart

The chakra associated with love and compassion is located in the middle of the chest, just above the heart. The color is green.

An imbalance in the heart chakra can manifest in people putting others' needs before their own to the extent that they harm themselves. It also stands for connection to other people with its location in the middle of the seven chakras. An imbalance could bring feelings of isolation and insecurity. Physically, heart problems, asthma, and weight gain are associated with the heart chakra (Stelter, 2016).

The Fifth Chakra: The Throat

With its color of vibrant blue, it represents verbal communication, and the associated organs such as the mouth, teeth, gums, and vocal cords.

A blockage or problem with balance can manifest in physical problems in these areas, as well as hesitant or malicious communication (Stelter, 2016).

The Sixth Chakra: The Third Eye or Brow

It is located between the eyes and the associated color is indigo. It represents imagination and intuition, as well as physical conditions of the head.

A blockage can show itself through headaches, eye, or ear problems. People who are out of touch with their intuition, or who seem to live in their own world where they "know everything," can be suffering from a problem with the sixth chakra (Stelter, 2016).

The Seventh Chakra: The Crown

Spiritual awareness and intelligence are associated with this chakra and its color is violet or white.

The crown chakra links the other chakras and is associated with the nervous system and brain.

People who stubbornly cling to narrow-minded views or drift aimlessly through life, always searching for their true purpose, might have an imbalance here (Stelter, 2016).

Exercise 5: The Role of Sound

There are two ways of healing chakras and removing blockages with sound. It can be done by voice or with tuning forks.

A different vowel is associated with each chakra and the voice can chant the specific vowel sound to balance a chakra.

To find the pitch for every chakra, use the same technique applied earlier in the resonance exercises. Choose a pitch and feel if it resonates in the region where the targeted chakra is. If not, move your pitch up or down until you feel the energy moving in the right place. A rule of thumb is that the lower chakras vibrate to lower pitches.

There is no need to chant loudly.

Focus your intention of balancing and clearing the specific chakra into your voice. Sit comfortably and keep your spine as straight as possible to allow energy to move freely.

Gently tone every sound seven times on your breath without forcing anything.

- The root: The sound is a deep, guttural 'uuh,' as in the word 'duck.'
- The sacral: The sound is 'ooh', as in the word 'do.'
- The solar plexus: The sound is 'ohh', as in the word 'low.'
- The heart: The sound is 'aah', as in the word 'ta.'
- The throat: The sound is 'eye', as in the word 'rye.'

- The third eye/brow: The sound is 'ay', as in the word 'bay.'
- The crown: The sound is 'eee', as in the word 'bee.'

Instead of using the balancing vowels, the chakra bija, or seed, mantras can also be chanted. Every chakra has its own bija mantra that represents the primordial time of creation.

- The root: The sound is 'lam.'
- The sacral: The sound is 'vam.'
- The solar plexus: The sound is 'ram.'
- The heart: The sound is 'yam.'
- The throat: The sound is 'ham.'
- The third eye/brow: The sound is 'aum.'
- The crown: The sound is 'om.'

Afterward, sit quietly for at least 10 minutes to experience the flow of energy. If you feel lightheaded at all when getting up, do an 'aah' to bring your energy down to the heart, and then an 'ooh' to ground yourself again properly (Wakeling, 2007).

Balancing the chakras using tuning forks requires more specialized knowledge and is usually done by practitioners qualified in sound healing. The chakras correspond to specific frequencies and the tuning forks have to be placed on the chakra that is being treated in specific intervals and combinations.

This interacts with what has become known as the biofield of a person. The term biofield refers to the sum of the energetic body that surrounds every human being. The term was coined in 1992 by researchers and practitioners in the Office of Alternative Medicine at the US National Institutes of Health, which is now the National Center for Complementary and Alternative Medicine (Rubik et al., 2015).

When a person's body is in balance, all the frequencies are in harmony. An organ or system that goes out of balance, brings dissonance in this harmonic world. With the aid of tuning forks, the dissonant body part is gently brought back to the right frequency and the sense of unease disappears.

The chakras correspond to the same solfeggio frequencies that were discussed in an earlier chapter (Weller, 2020).

- The root: 396 Hz.
- The sacral: 417 Hz.
- The solar plexus: 528 Hz.
- The heart: 639 Hz.
- The throat: 741 Hz.
- The third eye/brow: 852 Hz.
- The crown: 963 Hz.

SHAMAN SOUND HEALING WITH INSTRUMENTS

The rituals and sounds used by shamans worldwide bring another dimension to healing. A shamanic ceremony aims to alter consciousness, putting someone in a trance state where healing and balancing can take place, and an openness to receive wisdom and answers to specific questions a person might have is created. The shaman him/herself also enters into a trance and journeys to other worlds.

This is done by using various instruments such as drums, rattles, and Australian didgeridoos, as well as employing the voice of the shaman and sometimes the client's too, depending on whether it is an active or passive session.

Shamanic drumming is perhaps the most well-known. Researchers have found rapid drumming of about 220 beats per minute to be a vehicle for putting a person in a trance. The frequency range correlates with theta brain waves, at 3 to 8 Hz (Gingras et al., 2014).

Goldman and Sims explain the effect of drumming in terms of what is called auditory driving. Drumming stimulates the brain's reticular activating system (RAS). The primary function of the RAS is to regulate electrical activity in the brain. After a while of strong, repetitive drumming, the RAS gets overwhelmed and all other stimuli are ignored. That frees the shaman's mind to travel to other worlds and communicate with spirit beings and animals (2016).

Exercise 6: Using Your Voice as a Drum

It might not be possible to attend a session with a shaman, but you can create the same beneficial brain state for yourself by using your voice.

To mimic the sound of a drum, you can start with a 'kuh' sound, as in the word 'cup.' Inhale comfortably and exhale on the sound of 'kuh.' Keep the initial rhythm to one beat per second until you find your innate sense of rhythm. Gradually speed it up to a fast pace, keeping it going for about a minute. Notice any difference in energy you might feel.

Slow right down again, to about one beat every two to three seconds. Keep this also up for a minute and be aware of your nervous system and heartbeat slowing down in time with the rhythm.

You can repeat the exercise with a 'boom' sound and notice if it makes you feel more grounded, in contrast to the energizing effect of the 'kuh' sound.

❀ 4 ❀

FROM POLLUTION TO PANACEA

Cities are never quiet, not even at night.

M odern life offers very few opportunities for stillness and quality quiet time if we don't look for it on purpose. The everyday sounds we are exposed to constantly are often more damaging to our health than we might realize, both in their volume and their essence.

Blaring televisions, bleeping computers, and smartphones with a variety of ringtones all demand ongoing attention from our brains. This creates a stressful situation in the body.

NOISE POLLUTION

Noise pollution can be described as any noise we perceive as intruding on our thoughts and activities. It could be as loud as the club down the street, or as soft as the audible conversation of the people sitting at the next table in the restaurant.

A couple of sounds have been identified as the main culprits that have a significant negative impact on people's health. They are airplanes, traffic, noisy workplaces, and incessant household sounds (Scott, 2020).

Healthy Sound Levels

The human ear can get damaged by either one very loud sound or sounds over a period of time that are continuously higher than what scientists have determined to be a safe range to protect hearing.

Sound is measured in decibels (dB). Breathing measures at about 10 dB, a whisper is about 30 dB, and normal conversation is between 55 and 60 dB.

When the sound level creeps up to 70 dB, such as a washing machine or a dishwasher, slight annoyance might start to creep in. Traffic noise from inside a car can get up to 85 dB, which is significantly more annoying to the people in the vehicle.

Any sound louder than 70 dB that is sustained over a long time can cause permanent damage to someone's hearing.

Exposure to the sound of a motorcycle engine running at full speed and measuring at 95 dB can cause some hearing loss after only 50 minutes. Only 15 minutes of listening to a sound at 100 dB, such as an approaching subway train, will cause damage.

The sound levels in venues such as bars and nightclubs can get as high as 110 dB and after only two minutes' exposure, a measure of hearing loss can occur.

Any sound louder than 120 dB will cause immediate pain and ear injury, possibly resulting in permanent hearing loss (National Center for Environmental Health, 2019).

THE EFFECTS OF NOISE POLLUTION

The World Health Organization (WHO) considers noise pollution to be the second most dangerous environmental threat to human health, behind air pollution. The European Environment Agency (EEA) estimates that long-term exposure to high levels of environmental noise causes 12,000 premature deaths and 48,000 new cases of ischemic heart disease in Europe annually. They also point the finger to noise for more than 72,000 hospitalizations for a variety of causes every year in Europe alone (EEA, n.d.).

The negative impact of excessive noise lies in the fact that it raises our stress levels, even if it is only subconscious. This triggers the release of stress hormones such as cortisol. While cortisol is essential in body processes such as the metabolizing of glucose, secretion of insulin, and regulating of the immune response, sustained high levels of the hormone have been shown many times to be harmful to the human body.

Warning signs of harmful cortisol levels include blood sugar problems, elevated blood pressure, brain fog, increased abdominal fat, suppressed thyroid function, slow wound healing, and low immunity (Scott, 2021).

Under normal circumstances, the body's 'off switch' kicks in after an acute stressor has passed and cortisol production decreases again. When stress is chronic, as in the case of environmental noise, the de-stressing signal does not get a chance to activate.

Aircraft

The engine sound of a modern passenger aircraft can reach up to 140 dB during takeoff.

A study undertaken by various European scientists found that aircraft noise can cause significant health problems. Besides disrupting sleep and hampering academic performance in children, people living close to airports were vulnerable to cardiac disease, elevated blood pressure, obesity due to increased stress hormones, and lower birth weight in newborns.

Psychologically, people complained of poor quality of life, anxiety, and depression (Basner et al., 2017).

An Australian study compared the effect of noise pollution caused by aircraft on memory and recall to the effects of drinking too much alcohol. After being exposed to simulated aircraft noise at 65 dB, their scores in an auditory recall exercise showed the same deterioration as they did after the participants were administered alcohol under monitored conditions until their blood alcohol concentration measured 0.10 (Molesworth et al., 2013). This level is double the legal limit imposed in many countries to drive a car.

Passengers inside the airplane cabins are not safe from possible noise pollution either. During an assessment of the noise levels within a number of modern passenger airplanes, the median level of sound was found to be 83.5 dB. The full range of sound measured was between 37.6 dB and 110 dB and exposure varied with seating positions. Being closer to the engines, for example in seats in line with the wings, aggravated the situation (Zevitas et al., 2018).

Traffic

The WHO classifies road and railroad traffic as the second most harmful form of environmental pollution. Only air pollution is deemed to be worse (EEA, n.d.).

The stress responses provoked in the body by traffic noise do not even get turned off or lessened during sleep. Vehicle engines, tires, and road surfaces all combine to deliver a constant bombardment of sound levels above 55 dB. This has led one Danish technology company to describe traffic noise in one of their reports, quite aptly, as a slow death (Finne & Petersen, n.d.).

In another study conducted in Denmark, it was found that the risk for developing high blood pressure increased by 6% when noise levels experienced in the home increased by 10 dB. The risk of a stroke increased by 11% (Sørensen et al., 2013).

Workplaces

Earplugs are not always the best solution to cancel out the noise in an office.

Besides the obvious pictures of construction sites and factories that come to mind, other work environments can be just as harmful in terms of the sound levels experienced.

Symptoms of noise-related problems can include frequent headaches, persistent irritability without an apparent cause, increasing stress, dizziness, unexplained increases in blood pressure and/or heart rate, frequent and uncharacteristic mistakes and work accidents, and trouble discerning someone's words when there are other sounds. In addition to this, wearing earplugs to minimize distractions could lead to diminished productivity due to incidents such as missed phone calls.

Office workers who listen to their own music through earphones could damage their hearing even more if the volume is turned up too high for too long.

The open office model is very popular in large offices but it could be detrimental to employees. A busy office can easily reach a sound level of 50 dB. That is not only distracting but can also significantly increase stress levels and the accompanying health risks.

Households and Shopping Malls

Outdoor noise levels can also increase indoor levels. It becomes increasingly difficult to enjoy music or hear a phone conversation when traffic is roaring outside the window, for instance.

A French study done on the homes of 44 schoolchildren over eight months found them to be exposed to constant sounds such as television sets, music playing, cleaning equipment, cooking utensils and equipment, ventilation systems, freezers, and pets. The combined effect pushed the households' overall sound level several times during a 24 hour period higher than the level recommended by the European Environmental Agency (Pujol et al., 2014).

The Effects on Animals

The animal kingdom also suffers as a result of our noisy civilization. Many geographical surveys have shown a decline in births for many species in noisy environments.

Whales and dolphins are also greatly impacted by ocean noise caused by ship traffic, oil drills, sonar equipment, and seismic testing (National Geographic Society, 2019).

HOW TO TURN THE NOISE TIDE

It is impossible to avoid or stop all sounds that are too loud, so we have to learn to live with them and make them work in our favor whenever we can.

Limit the Noise

The first and probably most obvious solution would be to limit the amount of noise that reaches our living and working environment.

Physical steps to help you achieve this can include installing double window panes, applying weatherstripping to doors and windows, adding insulation on the ceilings, and installing sound-proofing panels to your working and sleeping areas, if not the whole house or office. These methods are costly, however, and can be quite invasive and disruptive for work and home routines during installation.

Start Over

Sometimes the only solution will be to move away from the job or area with unacceptable noise levels.

Although it is a drastic step, it is worth considering if it is possible for you. It could turn out to be the best gift you have given yourself in a long time.

Do Damage Control

We are not always able to control our environments and the amounts of noise we have to endure on a daily basis. Fortunately, there are ways to limit the damage and reverse the detrimental effects to recover your mental equilibrium and inner harmony.

Spend time in meditation and do some yoga stretches. Remember to breathe deeply and calmly—especially when you detect stress anywhere in your body. Taking a minute out to do a breathing exercise will bring amazing and quick changes.

Combine meditation with a mantra or chanting when you can to balance your vibrations and bring your body and mind back into harmony. Use good sounds to counteract bad sounds.

Replace the Noise

Fill your working and living space with soothing sounds to cancel out the noise. There are several online sources to find soundscapes from nature for free. Running rivers, booming ocean waves, rustling leaves, crackling fires—whatever combination of sounds resonates with you will be available to play, or sometimes to download, at only the cost of the data.

White, pink, brown, and blue noise can also be found in abundance online and in mobile applications.

The trusty pair of headphones to play your favorite music should not be forgotten either. Just remember to keep the volume low enough to protect your hearing.

Improve Creativity With Volume

In a 2012 experiment, a group of scientists found that people performing specific tasks with a soundtrack playing in the background at a consistent 70 dB performed better than those who worked in complete silence. That is the same sound level found in a typical busy coffee shop or restaurant (Mehta et al., 2012). Volumes lower or higher than 70 dB did not lead to good performance either.

It seems sound levels have a sweet spot where creativity is concerned and if we harness that, sounds that could have been deemed noise pollution can work to our benefit.

The science behind this insight started in the 1950s, with a psychologist called J. P. Guilford. He distinguished between the processes of divergent and convergent thinking, to arrive at a creative solution to a problem.

During the divergent phase, all the possibilities are examined. When the best one is chosen, the convergent phase zooms in on it and makes it take shape.

Sometimes our creative processes seem to fail because we skip the divergent step or don't consider enough different options. That is where a sound environment of 70 dB comes in: That is just enough to keep us from concentrating so intently on a problem that we narrow the field before it has a chance to develop.

The type of sound is important, however. Only steady streams of jumbled familiar sounds will stimulate our creative cognitive processes, such as indistinct chatter or ocean waves. One-sided phone conversations and even white or pink noise won't do the trick.

These types of sounds are usually lower-pitched than isolated voices or phones and we perceive the vibrations to be more relaxing, thereby stimulating our creativity.

Use Sonic Transmutation

The concept of transmuting something implies that a sound is being turned into something else—something that is useful instead of annoying.

The ancient Egyptians understood this principle already when they built the pyramids. These fascinating triangular shapes that have mesmerized people ever since seem to have been used for more than burial sites.

Besides being sites to send deceased kings into the afterlife with everything they will need, archaeologists believe the design of the pyramids was also used to benefit the living.

Scientific experiments conducted in the Great Pyramid of Giza, which was built as a tomb for the pharaoh Khufu, showed the design of the pyramid could collect electromagnetic waves and concentrate them in specific points. This fact, coupled with the highly resonant qualities of the walls because of the high quartz content in the limestone, has led some scientists to conclude the pyramids were also used as places of healing, maybe during worship rituals (Balezin et al., 2018).

Egyptians thought seven of their vowel sounds were sacred. During rituals, the priests chanted these vowels in a convergent harmony that reverberated from the walls of structures such as pyramids.

Acoustic physics researcher John Stuart Reid conducted a cymatics experiment in the late 1990s to show the resonant power of the Great Pyramid by using an oscillator and a speaker arrangement that mimicked the vowel chant of the priests.

Many of the images he observed in the patterns formed by the quartz crystals he used in his experiment resembled Egyptian hieroglyphs. This led Reid to surmise that the ancient writing incorporated harmonies too.

Based on this experiment and others that followed, Egyptologists believe the measurements and angles on which the pyramids were built were designed to produce maximum resonance for the chanting sounds. The rituals were used to heal and, after death, to send the body of the king off to the stars to be reborn.

The patterns contained in the hieroglyphs were carried over through the years to come but, sadly, we lost the knowledge of the harmonies that accompanied them (Cymascope, n.d.).

CRYSTALS

Gemstones used in natural healing.

Crystals can be a great aid in turning the noise tide. There are hundreds of different types available, each with its own vibration and area of benefit.

Gemstones have been used since ancient times to heal diseases and soothe troubled minds. When the power of the crystals is magnified with sound, they become even more effective.

A Brief History

Crystals are first mentioned by the Sumerians. They were an ancient Mesopotamian people who are credited with starting civil life in the way we modern humans understand a civilization to be. They included various crystals in their formulas for magic processes and potions.

The Egyptians put great stock in the power of stones such as lapis lazuli, turquoise, emerald, and carnelian. They used them as jewelry, as well as to treat the sick. Green stones were seen as symbols of a deceased heart and were used in burial rituals.

The ancient Greeks knew and used several gemstones and many of the names for gemstones we know today are of Greek origin. They used stones for protection and healing.

Jade was valuable in old China and emperors and other powerful people were sometimes buried in suits of armor made from jade.

The tradition of green stones being seen as lucky continues to this day in some parts of the world, for instance, in New Zealand.

Most religions also use and value gemstones in some form. Their importance has waxed and waned with the trends in society and scientific developments.

In the 1980s, interest in New Age philosophies picked up and gemstones and crystals were rediscovered as healing tools and emotional aids. It is still not accepted by mainstream medical science as a valid healing tool but crystal therapy is used by many people to enhance their lives and health.

How Does It Work?

Crystals, like any other part of the universe, vibrate at specific frequencies that give them their physical makeup and appearance. Some frequencies are the same as some of our organs and emotions and by enhancing a positive vibration, it is believed that disease can be healed and emotions can be balanced and calmed.

Healers see themselves as mere conduits for the healing vibrations, channeling them to the person receiving the therapy.

The roots of crystal healing therapy lie in Chinese and Indian culture, with the concepts of qi and the chakras.

Cleansing and Recharging Your Crystals With Sound

Most crystals are believed to absorb the negative energy they remove from the body and mind, as well as any energy around them when they are transported or stored. They have to be cleansed occasionally to continue to be of benefit in healing.

There are several ways to do this but not all of them work for all crystals. Sound cleansing and charging is one method that will be effective on any type of crystal.

It is not difficult to do and cannot damage your crystals. Any resonating object that can hold the tone for ten minutes or more can be used, such as tuning forks and singing bowls.

Singing bowls are well suited to this because their high copper content ensures they keep their tone ringing for as long as they are in use. They are positioned on a cushion to prolong the bell-like sound even further.

Cleansing with the bowls is a practical way to clean a whole array of crystals at once, or cleaning and charging big crystals that cannot be moved easily.

The size of the bowl does not matter that much. Smaller bowls emit a higher-pitched sound than larger ones but both sides of the sound spectrum will do what is needed for your crystals.

Be sure not to buy decorated or painted bowls when you shop for new ones. The paint hides the copper and dulls, or even changes the sound. It will also cause the sound to stop quickly instead of continuing its ringing for some time after being struck with its special wooden stick. If the bowl is made of the wrong metal or the wrong composition of metals, the ringing will also stop quickly and the sound might be more similar to hitting a regular saucepan with a wooden spoon.

Arrange your crystals around the bowl but never put them inside. The movements caused by the vibration of the bowl will make the stones hit against the metal insides of the bowl and each other. That can chip or otherwise damage your crystals, especially the softer or brittle ones.

Cleansing Smaller Crystals With a Singing Bowl

- Place the bowl on its cushion after making sure the cushion rests flat on a hard and stable surface.
- Arrange the crystals to be cleansed and recharged around the cushion. Make sure no stones touch the bowl.

- Strike the outside of the bowl gently with the wooden stick to start its ringing sound.
- Rub the outside of the bowl with the wooden stick in a clockwise direction to sustain the ringing. Apply some pressure to the rubbing but keep it gentle.
- Hold your intention of purifying and recharging the crystals in mind while keeping up the rubbing.
- You can amplify the ringing sound by humming along with it if you want.
- Keep rubbing until you feel your intention has been communicated.

Cleansing the Larger Stones With a Singing Bowl

- Stand as close to your crystals as you can.
- Hold the bowl on the flat palm of your non-dominant hand.
- If possible, hold your hand with the bowl over the crystals or right next to them.
- Take the wooden stick in your other hand and strike the side of the bowl gently to start the ringing.
- Follow the rest of the steps outlined in the section above.

Recharging and Retuning Your Crystals With Tuning Forks

The same sound effect can be created by using a good-sized tuning fork. The sound should be loud enough to penetrate the structure of the crystal to move its molecules and realign them to their own powerful vibrations.

The specific note struck does not matter, as long as it is loud enough and can be sustained while sending your intention to the crystals.

- If you want to recharge your crystals with a specific

frequency, you can consider using what is known as a crystal tuner. It is a tuning fork designed to resonate at 4,096 Hz. This is said to be the frequency of quartz as well as of the earth. Proponents of crystal tuners believe the pure frequency creates a bridge between the energies of heaven and earth when the ringing tuner is touched against a crystal.

Tap the tuning fork gently in your hand, on a hard surface, or with a rubber mallet to start it ringing. Hold the vibrating tuning fork over the crystal you are retuning for as long as you feel it is needed while sending your clear intention to it.

Recharging Crystals With Tingshas

Traditional Buddhist tingshas.

Tibetan tingshas are sets of tiny copper cymbals joined by a leather thong. Buddhists have used them for centuries as traditional aids in prayers and ceremonies.

Tingshas emit a high-pitched sound that can be sustained for quite some time. The etymology of the name refers to its sustaining power—'ting' mimics the sound of the metal, while 'sha' means 'hanging' in the Tibetan language.

Retuning Your Crystals With Vocal Toning

Vocal toning does not need a high note. You only need sustained sound at some degree of audible volume to move the molecules of the crystal. The louder your tone, the faster the molecules will vibrate to speed up the process.

Hold the crystal to be tuned in front of your mouth and take a deep, relaxed diaphragm breath. Imagine you are inhaling something with the power to purify and energize. Give a form and a color to this purifying energy.

Exhale the purifying energy slowly over the crystal, carrying it on your voice on any pitch that is comfortable for you. Don't think about the note before singing it, allow the note that comes naturally at that moment and sustain it on your exhalation as long as you can.

Visualize your voice and the purifying sound wrapping around the crystal.

Keep toning until you feel you want to shift your pitch higher or lower. When that shift occurs, you will know the crystal is retuned and ready.

The Power of Music and the Voice

Never underestimate the powerful effect that your own voice and the vibrations the sound of it creates, which are like signatures of your true self, can have when used with pure intentions.

Whether you sing, speak, or chant, your intention of recharging and realigning the crystal to yourself and your needs makes the difference.

Even just singing along to a favorite piece of music with a joyful and pure heart can accomplish everything your crystals need. Not all of us have the talents or available time of monks; use what you have and do it with enthusiasm and purity.

A Reprogramming Visualization for Crystals

In this visualization exercise, the spoken word is combined with an intention to create an effortless re-tuning for your crystals.

- Stand in natural light, outside, or at a window.
- Hold the crystal to be recharged in your left hand. Your left side is the receiving side of your body.
- If you want to, you can play music at a frequency of your

choice in the background. If your purpose is to dedicate the stone for a specific use, you can choose the frequency that boosts that aspect of life.

- Breathe deeply and calmly for a couple of seconds to center yourself, while being sensitive to the weight and the sensations of the crystal in your hand.
- While gazing with love and gratitude at the crystal, say aloud, "I dedicate this crystal to be used for my highest good and truest purposes. I welcome its energy into my life. I ask to receive its love and light."
- If you want the crystal's assistance with something specific, form that intention and your mind and speak it aloud toward the crystal. It could be anything from opening your heart up to finding a life partner to helping you heal from disease.
- Finish by saying aloud, "I now dedicate this crystal to... (your chosen purpose for the stone)".
- If it is practical to do, you can wear the reprogrammed crystal against your body for seven days to settle the new energy. Bigger crystals should be touched regularly in the week following the visualization.

A Cleansing Meditation for Crystals

For this meditation, you can either put your crystals in your lap or just visualize them in your mind's eye.

Sit comfortably with your feet next to each other on the floor, ankles uncrossed, and arms and hands resting calmly in your lap.

If you are holding crystals in your lap, you can rest your hands on them if you want.

Play a soundscape of your choice in the background or use music in the universal transformation frequency of 528 Hz.

Close your eyes if you are comfortable doing that and breathe in deeply but comfortably, feeling your abdomen swelling with the air drawn deeply into your body.

Breathe out until your stomach and rib cage are completely flat again.

Experience the stillness and serenity in and around you and bathe your spirit in it.

Breathe in serenity...and breathe out inner chatter.

And breathe in serenity...and breathe out inner chatter.

Picture your crystals in your mind.

Visualize a pure white light shining down to envelop you and the stones in energizing warmth.

Savor the warmth for a while.

Breathe in energy...and breathe out exhaustion.

And breathe in energy...and breathe out exhaustion.

[Pause for as long as you want in this feeling].

Now see the white light gently washing every crystal, removing any negative energy and stagnant experience.

See the brilliant colors of every gemstone reemerging to sparkle in the healing white light.

Breathe in purity...and breathe out stagnant energy.

And breathe in purity...and breathe out stagnant energy.

Keep on doing the spiritual wash until you intuitively feel your crystals are cleansed and recharged.

See the white light gently washing every crystal, removing any negative energy and stagnant experience.

Enjoy the brilliant sparkle of the colors in every crystal, playing in the healing white light.

Breathe in purity...and breathe out stagnant energy.

And breathe in purity...and breathe out stagnant energy.

When you are ready, become aware of your surroundings again and open your eyes.

Hold the recharged crystals for a while and allow their vibrations to move you.

CHOOSING THE RIGHT CRYSTALS

You can be forgiven if you feel fairly bewildered by the vast variety of crystals and gemstones available to choose from. Each one has an area it specializes in and the colors are also important.

It does not fall within the scope of this book to discuss all the criteria for choosing crystals. We are concerned with sound healing and some crystals will resonate stronger than others.

To gather a beginner's set of stones, consider getting clear quartz, rose quartz, citrine, amethyst, black tourmaline, tiger's eye, aquamarine, green calcite, pyrite, and pink opal.

Clear Quartz

Clear quartz is known as the master healer. It is believed to balance mind, body, and soul. It also supercharges intentions, making it a great aid for beginners.

It not only amplifies its own energy but also boosts the energy of any crystals used alongside it.

Rose Quartz

This beautiful pink gemstone is known as the queen of self-love, relationships, and harmony.

It is credited with strengthening emotional and sexual bonds between partners, enhancing harmony, and neutralizing conflicts.

Citrine

The bright yellow of citrine awakens personal power. It also helps to get rid of negative energy and will provide a boost of confidence and conviction to people in stressful careers.

Amethyst

Amethyst is used to bring calm in a hectic schedule and relieve stress while enhancing spiritual connections, insights, and intuition, as well as opening the third eye.

Many healers use amethyst to get rid of addictions. Ancient Greeks carved their drinking vessels from amethyst in the belief that drinking from them would prevent intoxication.

Black Tourmaline

This stone is used as a powerful protector against negativity and people wanting to drain your personal energy.

It is also used to calm anxiety and balance the right and left sides of the brain.

Placing a black tourmaline crystal near electronic equipment can also mitigate the effect of electromagnetic waves on our energy levels and block some of the energy drain.

Tiger's Eye

Tiger's eye is used to ground a person. It can boost physical performance.

The stone also enhances focus and motivates you to take advantage of all the opportunities offered by the universe.

Aquamarine

This is the best stone to turn to when you find it difficult to speak your truth and stay true to yourself. It helps you to set boundaries without aggression or apology and guides you in tense conversations.

Aquamarine also boosts creativity.

Green Calcite

Green calcite helps us to get rid of blocks and obstacles to personal growth. It cleans our energy and amplifies the benefits.

Due to its green color, it is also strongly associated with prosperity and abundance.

Pyrite

Pyrite is used as a protector on all levels, from energetic to spiritual to physical. It is also said to boost manifesting when the crystal is used during meditation.

Pink Opal

Pink opal helps to release anger and tension, restoring calm and serenity. It also helps to relieve anxiety and insomnia.

It works on a subconscious level to heal old emotional wounds and release any lingering trauma and pain.

DOES SIZE MATTER?

The size of your crystal does not change the type of energy it can provide. A big chunk of the gemstone will pack a more powerful punch that will affect you quicker but the essential outcome will remain the same, whether the crystal is big or small.

HOW DO YOU MAKE A CHOICE?

It is often said that a person is chosen by a crystal and not the other way round.

Some crystals will 'speak' to you if you need them at that point in your life. Touching various crystals for a few moments with your eyes closed will quickly detect a vibrational reaction.

UNLOCKING YOUR MERIDIANS
WITH SOUND

Meridians are concepts from traditional Chinese medicine (TCM). They are to chakras as railway lines are to stations—they form the channels along which energy travels through the body, to arrive at the various centers where it is concentrated for specific purposes.

The physical existence of meridians has not been proved yet, but practitioners of the system firmly believe in them and use them to heal and restore.

TCM is an ancient medical system that has been around for almost 4,000 years.

KEY CONCEPTS IN TCM

The first concept to understand is qi. That refers to the invisible energy force that is life itself. In the literal sense, the Chinese word means 'air.'

TCM believes illness occurs whenever anything obstructs the free flow of qi through the body. The system of coordinated movements, breathing techniques, and meditation traditionally used to balance and maintain qi is called qigong.

The meridians through which the qi circulates are divided into two parts. The jingmai contains the main meridians, while the luomai contains the associated vessels such as the arteries.

Every meridian exists as a part of a pair. One is yin in nature and the other is yang. In TCM, yin corresponds to cold, darkness, and water. Yang corresponds to daylight, heat, and fire (Fellows, n.d.).

THE MERIDIANS

There are 12 main meridians. They run on each side of the body and each meridian relates to an organ. The two sides mirror each other.

The meridians are the liver, gallbladder, heart, small intestine, spleen, stomach, lung, large intestine, kidney, urinary bladder, San Jiao, and Pericardium. The San Jiao meridian is also known as the triple burner and helps to regulate organs and energy, in the same way Western medicine understands metabolism. Its nature is yang. The pericardium meridian is the cardiovascular meridian and it has a yin nature (Traditional Chinese Medicine World Foundation, 2019).

The Liver Meridian

The liver is essential for a healthy metabolism with its function of digesting nutrients. In TCM, it is also associated with frustration, irritability, bitterness, depression, and sadness.

Physical symptoms that can manifest when this meridian is blocked include dizziness, dry eyes and other vision-related problems, dental issues, sinusitis, period pains, diseases of the reproductive system, and fatigue.

The Gallbladder Meridian

The gallbladder produces bile that helps with the detoxification of the body. In TCM, it is associated with rage.

Physical signs of a meridian problem include eye problems, hip, knee, and ankle joint problems, mouth ulcers, and pulmonary diseases.

The Heart Meridian

The heart is essential in providing life-giving oxygen to the body. It is seen as the seat of joy in TCM. Too little joy will result in depression, while too much joy will become manic.

Fearfulness, agitation, concentration difficulties, and resistance to forgiving people can manifest. Physical problems include heart palpitations and irregular heartbeat, as well as neuralgia of the arms and shoulders.

The Small Intestine Meridian

Magic happens inside the small intestine when food is converted into energy to fuel the body.

Psychologically, the small intestine meridian relates to the 'digestion' of mental and emotional issues. Prolonged feelings of grief and sadness without an apparent cause can result from a blocked or imbalanced small intestine meridian.

Symptoms of problems with this meridian include food allergies, all types of frequent infections, a tendency to incur strain injuries, skin diseases, and rheumatism.

The Spleen Meridian

The spleen forms part of the body's filter system. It removes bacteria, dead blood cells, and any other impurities.

A tendency to worry in excess and dwell almost obsessively on one topic is an emotional sign of problems with this meridian.

Physically, loss of appetite, exhaustion, bloating, diarrhea, and blood disorders can point to spleen meridian dysfunction.

The Stomach Meridian

The stomach is not only the place where physical food is digested, but it also represents the digesting of ideas. Problems with the stomach meridian can show themselves as an inability to assimilate new ideas and incorporate them into your life.

The stomach meridian runs up to the top of the head and can also manifest in sinus irritations, tooth problems, facial palsy, thyroid issues, and lymph blockages.

Psychologically, depression, bitterness, and a constant, gnawing sense of hunger can be experienced.

The Lung Meridian

Without the lungs' ability to take in oxygen from the outside world and convert it into life-giving breath, we'd die. The lung meridian also represents communication with the outside world and our willingness to live life fully.

Allergies, skin problems, asthma, sweating, kidney problems, and digestive issues can indicate a blocked lung meridian.

Extreme worrying, feeling detached and overwhelmed, and having a scornful, intolerant disposition can indicate problems with the lung meridian.

The Large Intestine Meridian

The large intestine is situated at the end of the food's journey through our bodies. The associated meridian also represents our final evaluation of our life experiences.

Constant feelings of guilt and a lack of self-esteem and a healthy self-image result when the large intestine meridian is blocked.

On a physical level, sinusitis, joint pain, rheumatic conditions, bronchitis, skin diseases, and stomach problems can be present.

The Kidney Meridian

In TCM, the kidneys relate to fear. A blockage in this meridian can show itself through fearfulness and anxiety, as well as aloofness which results from feeling insecure.

Possible diseases include chronic ear infections, non-age-related problems with eyesight, lower back problems, bone marrow and bone density issues, incontinence, prostate, and reproductive problems.

The Urinary Bladder Meridian

This is the longest meridian, running from the top of the head to the soles of the feet. In TCM, it has a close connection to the kidney meridian. Infections from sinusitis to chronic cystitis can therefore occur when this meridian is blocked.

In addition, eye and ear diseases, sciatica, and issues with the reproductive system can be experienced.

The emotions expressed can include acute restlessness, frustration, and impatience.

The San Jiao/Triple Burner Meridian

All hormonal glands are included in this meridian. It represents our inspiration to act powerfully and energetically.

Fever or shivers, headaches, and a sore throat can result from an imbalance or blockage in this meridian.

Feelings of despair, hopelessness, loneliness, and isolation can be experienced.

The Pericardium Meridian

A person's zest for life and his/her level of motivation are closely connected to this meridian in TCM. The libido is also linked.

Possible diseases include heart and angina problems, feelings of pressure in the heart area, pain in the lung area, spasms, bad blood circulation, hernias, and gastritis.

On the psychological level, a blockage here can result in manic emotional episodes, delirium, and experiencing a lack of joy in life in general.

OPENING THE FLOW OF QI WITH SOUND

The Chinese developed a system called Qigong to clear blockages and balance meridians to ensure qi flows freely through the body.

A Brief History

Qigong dates back more than 4,000 years. It has roots in Chinese culture, philosophy, medicine, and martial arts. It involves slow, coordinated movements, sounds, and meditation.

Liu Guizhen is the man credited with giving the system its name. In 1947, at 27 years of age, Guizhen was sent home to his village from his job as a clerk for the Communist Party, to die. He suffered from tuberculosis and nervous problems, as well as severe gastric ulcers. He weighed less than 80 pounds.

His uncle claimed to know the secrets of a Buddhist tradition called Neiyang gong and decided to teach his nephew how to practice it, to save his life.

The next 100 days under the guidance of his uncle were grueling. Guizhen was not allowed to speak, wash, or receive visitors. He had to practice a series of movements every other waking hour and had to drink four to five thermos bottles of water per day, two of which had to be boiled water.

The exercises involved a lot of breathwork and mantras.

At the end of this period, Guizhen had gained 30 pounds and was a healthy man. He returned to work, much to the amazement of the Communist officials. They were eager to learn Guizhen's secret because China's people were suffering after the war and there were very few doctors.

He returned to his uncle and learned everything he could. His uncle told him the real secret was this: Chanting a silent mantra while focusing all the attention on a point below the navel slows down brain activity. That allows the organs to strengthen and heal of their own accord.

The communist party instructed Guizhen to standardize and simplify all the elements of the system and remove any religious and feudal connotations. They also changed the name to the more neutral word qigong, which has no roots in Buddhism.

In 1964, the official party line changed against qigong and the political leaders tried to eradicate the practice. Guizhen was imprisoned and the institutions where it was practiced closed.

Its popularity was revived in 1978 and has endured to this day (Voigt, 2013).

Qigong Today

The emphasis in qigong has shifted from spiritual enlightenment to health and fitness. In China, it has been recognized as standard medical practice since 1989. In the Western tradition, it is still regarded as an alternative therapy to mainstream medicine.

The Five Elements

The original masters of qigong studied nature closely and concluded that the human body functions in synchronization to the elements and seasons found in nature.

The movements and the associated healing sounds were developed to bring the body gently back into the same rhythm as the earth's cycles to achieve balance.

They identified five elements and each one is associated with a season, color, sound, and system of organs (Flood, 2016).

Element	Organ	Color	Season	Sound
Wood	Liver	Green	Spring	Shoo
Fire	Heart	Red	Summer	Haaw
Earth	Spleen	Yellow	Late summer	Whoo
Metal	Lungs	White	Fall	Tzzz
Water	Kidneys	Blue	Winter	Ch-way
Triple Burner	Harmonizer			S-Hee (done silently)

An Exercise to Strengthen the Wood Element

The wood element represents energy for life, freedom, and high spirits. A strong presence of this element reflects creativity and flexibility.

Stand in the basic qigong stance, which is feet apart shoulder-width, knees slightly bent, and hands hanging loosely by the sides. The mouth should be closed with the tongue against the upper palate and the gaze should be fixed on the far horizon.

Put one foot forward and turn your body 90 degrees to the other side while swinging your arms along. Breathe in while you twist and exhale as you come back to the starting position (Isahak, 2005).

An Exercise to Strengthen the Fire Element

Our connection to ourselves and, from there, to everything else in the universe, is influenced by the strength of the fire element. It brings a calm and controlled life, filled with compassion for all beings.

This exercise starts with a meditative posture—lotus if you can, otherwise just sitting comfortably in a chair. Keep your hands resting comfortably on your knees with the palms facing upward.

Bring your heels together and fold your hands in front of your chest, in the Eastern greeting posture. Breathe in, then bend forward slightly while exhaling and contemplating compassion.

After four to six repeats of the movement, fold your arms and bend down fully while exhaling. Hold the position for a couple of moments while resolving to be more loving and tolerant (Isahak, 2005).

An Exercise to Strengthen the Earth Element

The earth element is interpreted as being about caring for oneself, others, and the environment.

Start with the basic stance. Bend one leg up behind you and grab that foot with both hands. Stretch the leg gently while breathing in. Exhale while relaxing and letting go of the foot, taking care to keep your balance (Isahak, 2005).

An Exercise to Strengthen the Metal Element

A harmonious metal element brings with it clarity of mind and freedom of prejudices and the ability to let go of emotions that no longer serve you.

Stand in the basic stance and lift your outstretched arms toward the sky, palms facing upward while breathing in. Lower your arms with the palms facing downward while exhaling.

Do four to six repetitions. On the last one, bend down completely as far as you can go while stretching your arms backward and locking your thumbs with the index fingers pointing up. Do three to six cycles of breathing in and out in this position.

Straighten up on the next inhalation with your arms pointing skyward again. Breathe out and bring your arms down the last time (Isahak, 2005).

An Exercise to Strengthen the Water Element

This element is about the self—who you are and where you are going.

Stand in the basic stance and raise your arms no higher than your waist with the palms turned outward. Keep your posture right with the lower spine as straight as possible and the upper spine relaxed without hunching over.

Visualize qi entering your body through the top of your head and flowing down your spine in a river of white light. Imagine the qi energizing your brain and spine and all the organs and body systems reached from the spine.

Next, sit down on the floor with your legs outstretched. Bend forward slightly while stretching your arms out with the palms facing upward. Breathe in and slowly swing your arms to the side as if you are swimming, and straighten your back again. Breathe out and bring your arms back to your chest.

Repeat the whole cycle four to six times (Isahak, 2005).

Using the Sounds

The sounds associated with each element, as shown in the table earlier in this section, can be incorporated with the exercises or used on their own.

There is a sound for each element and a sixth sound, to harmonize them all.

The tones should be made in a steady voice except for the sixth sound, which will be made silently and in the middle range of the voice where it is comfortable for you. Each sound should be repeated at least five times with the sixth one always last.

The order in which you do them is not important. You can also do only the one that is associated with an organ or system you are concerned about, or even do the one for the current season only.

The sounds create vibrations that act like a massage for the organs involved, thereby healing and stabilizing them.

There are no standardized movements with the sounds and many variations exist. The basic premise from which all of them start is that wood (trees) grow upward, fire moves in all directions, earth expands horizontally, metal contracts and holds, and water flows downward. You can improvise your own movements along these lines (Voigt, 2012).

The following section contains guidelines for the visualizations that should accompany each sound to make full use of its qualities. Remember that the organs don't correspond strictly with only the anatomical pinpoints we give to them. They refer to systems of organs.

In every instance, inhale as deeply as is comfortable through the nose and exhale while silently making the sound.

- Liver: While making the sound, use your imagination to guide the qi (white light) up from the inner sides of your big toes. Let it move up along the insides of the thighs, through the abdomen, and up to the throat. Allow the qi to move to the eyes, forehead, and right up to the crown of the head. Turn it back to move down into the lungs, flow down the inner sides of the arms, and end at the outer tips of the thumbs before inhaling.

- Heart: Imagine the qi starting on the outer sides of the big toes this time and moving up along the inner legs to enter the abdomen. From there, let it move to the upper chest, armpits, and flow along the inner arms, ending at the inside tips of the little fingers.

- Spleen: Start once again on the outer sides of the big toes and allow the qi to move up the inner sides of the legs into the abdomen. From there, guide the light to the stomach and then into the upper chest. Upon reaching the chest, imagine the qi dividing into two streams. The first stream brings the qi to the throat and lets it flow under the tongue. At the same time, the second stream moves the qi into the inner arms and allows it to flow down to the inside tips of the little fingers.

- Lungs: Starting the flow of the brilliant white light that is qi at the inner sides of the big toes, imagine it traveling up the inner legs and entering the abdomen. From there, let it move up into the lungs. The qi ends its round by flowing down the inner sides of the arms, ending at the inner tips of both thumbs.

- Kidney: From the balls of the feet, visualize the qi moving up through the inner thighs. Let it flow along the spine and enter the kidneys. Imagine it moving into the chest, before going down the inner arms and ending in the tips of the middle fingers.

- Triple burner: To harmonize and unite all the other sounds, visualize the qi starting at the outer tips of the fourth toes. See it moving up the outer legs into the sides of the torso. From there, allow the white light to flow to the sides of the neck and enter the head. Let it move back down again along the sides of the head, through the neck, over the shoulders, and along the backs of the arms, to end at the outside tips of the ring fingers (Voigt, 2012).

When you've done one set of exercises, you can repeat them while gently shaking your body. That is a natural way of getting rid of all trapped stress and concerns.

❧ 6 ❧

EMOTIONAL SOUND HEALING
SECRETS

We all go through an emotional dip at times. Some bouts of the blues occur after a specific traumatic or sad event but sometimes we are simply caught off guard by it.

In times like those it would be nice to have a magic solution but that's just wishful thinking. Or is it...?

Sound healing and balancing can make such a profound difference to your emotional and mental state that it can seem like magic.

If you think back to the introduction of this book for a moment, you will remember us talking about all particles of the universe, including those that make up our bodies, being in constant movement and vibration.

When something upsets this vibrational pattern, the cells retain a memory of the event and the energy becomes stagnant. That can cause long-term emotional problems.

Tuning in to the right sounds and music can erase the memory and restore the right balance needed for a happy, relaxed life.

THE RELATIONSHIP BETWEEN SOUND HEALING AND INTUITION

Intuition refers to our innate ability to perceive things directly from the universe. We are all born with it but as life progresses, we often choose to ignore intuition's messages to the point where it looks as if we lost the capability.

We never lose it, however, and with the right stimulation and the intention to allow intuition back into our lives, it can open up again and become our greatest ally in sound healing.

What is Intuition?

One of the most concise explanations of the nature of intuition can be found in the Japanese word for the concept. It consists of three written characters that represent directness, perception, and power.

When we allow our direct perception to be active, we once again become capable of discerning the truth in all matters, including the real roots of ailments and emotional upsets.

Intuition awakens our consciousness of being part of one source of creation that still unites all of us. There is one common thread flowing through all of creation: vibration.

Synchronicities and flashes of insight become commonplace and it gets much easier to reach the heart of any disease—whether in ourselves or others.

An active intuitive life raises our vibrations and it becomes easier to be in tune with positive emotions. That also makes it easier for a healer to distinguish between lighter, higher vibrations and the heavier, denser ones that are present in someone who needs healing.

Intuition and Music

The great Albert Einstein said that great scientists are artists too. True knowledge cannot exist without true, intuitive beauty.

The same is true about our health, and music is one of the best ways to awaken our intuitive road to complete wellness.

To Einstein, the only difference between science, including formal music, and intuition was the language in which the subject matter was presented. If it was expressed in terms of logic and formally accepted scientific concepts, it qualified as science. If it dealt with what he called "forms whose constructions are not accessible to the conscious mind but are recognized intuitively," Einstein grouped a project with intuition (Root-Bernstein & Root-Bernstein, 2010).

It is clear that music can access our essence at the base level and bring about positive changes if we allow it to.

THE ROLE OF INTENTION

Healing with sound is one of the most powerful healing modalities available to us but without the intention to heal, sound remains just another tool. A healing intention lifts the process to magical heights.

Sound healing expert Jonathan Goldman explains this in terms of a formula: Frequency + intent = healing (Goldman, 2009c).

While frequency represents the actual sound, Goldman describes intent as the energy behind the music or sound that gives it its power.

He goes on to relate a confusing experience in his authoring life when he was writing a book on the different mantras and sounds that are used in healing and their results. He noticed that all the gurus had different takes on which sound and mantra worked for which organ, and where each sound resonated. That did not make sense to Goldman because he was trying to compile a system for sound healing.

Then he experienced an aha-moment when he realized that all the experts get positive results because of their intentions. The sound and mantra are not the essential ingredients—the intention with which they are used is. All the healers intended to help their clients and facilitate their road back to optimum wellness, and those are the results they produced, regardless of where they felt resonance or which sound they used for an organ.

It is easy to prove this to yourself from everyday experiences. Have you ever met someone you haven't seen in a while and felt, after their enthusiastic greeting, that they would have preferred not to run into you?

We perceive the intention behind sounds on a subconscious level and we also respond to the intention on a subconscious level.

Goodman uses the example of a kinesiology experiment in which people's muscle strength was tested after listening to ocean sounds infused with good wishes from others, as well as wave sounds infused with anger and bad feelings by another group of people. While listening to the sounds that were infused with love, light, and happiness, the test participants' muscles stayed strong. When tested while listening to the "bad-vibed" ocean sounds, they became weak. Their physical structure and responses were influenced by the intentions caught up in the sounds they were listening to.

When working with sound, you can visualize the sound like a current coming to you. If you are the healer, your current has to be positive—but so too, if you are the receiver of a treatment. Energy follows intention because intention vibrates molecules.

BRAIN WAVE STATES

Our brains function through ongoing electrical impulses that measure only a few millionths of a volt. These waves vary with the different states our brains are in and the activities we are occupied with.

Five frequencies are widely used in scientific literature and can be measured on an EEG scan, as shown in the table below (Abhang et al., 2016).

Frequency	Brain State	Associated Activities
0.5–4 Hz	Delta	Sleeping; being in a deep trance
4–8 Hz	Theta	Deeply relaxed; focused; meditative; "in the zone"
8–12 Hz	Alpha	Passively attentive and very relaxed; observant
12–35 Hz	Beta	Alert but still relaxed, paying active attention to outside stimuli; anxiety-prone
35-80 Hz	Gamma	Deep concentration and hyper-focus; consciously paying attention and recalling memories

Brain wave patterns are as unique as fingerprints and can vary in different parts of the brain at the same time.

Low-frequency brain waves are activated when we listen to music and our brains and bodies synchronize themselves to the music.

This makes music one of the most powerful tools in a sound healing arsenal. It calms down the nervous system so that intuition can come through.

To prove this, Goldman explains his experience with shamans and other healers who are in deep trances, and their brain waves are measured at the delta frequency, during which they, theoretically, should have been asleep. They are, however, alert and talking, often channeling higher guidance in the trance state (2009c).

A MEDITATION TO SLOW DOWN

While listening to some calming music, such as can be found anywhere on websites such as YouTube, through earphones for the best effect, close your eyes and do the following short meditation to experience the calming effect of music while still concentrating and raising your vibrations.

Sit comfortably, or lie down, with the music swirling around you. Feel the music going through you.

Breathe in deeply and imagine taking the sound with your breath into your heart.

Exhale completely and visualize the music moving through your heart and out again, taking restlessness and frustration with it.

Do that a couple of times and feel your heart slowing down and the knot in your stomach loosening.

Now, think of anyone or anything you are grateful for. It could be a pet, a sibling, a partner, or something material such as your home.

Visualize the person, object, or place while breathing in the music...and out again.

Next, imagine a beautiful rose-gold cloud starting to form around you. See the cloud moving up and connecting to a huge rose-gold cloud from the universe.

See your cloud being carried on the sound of the music and merging with the universe's loving rose-gold cloud. Feel the peace of coming home and being loved and well.

Hold this oneness inside your mind for as long as the music is playing.

Open your eyes and carry the calm, loving, peaceful feeling with you as you go about the rest of your day.

OUR OWN MUSIC

All of us have music inside us. We can call upon our personal sounds in times of emotional turmoil if we would only realize they are there.

Heartbeats, sighs, and breathing are all forms of sound therapy that are freely available to us. If you know how to utilize them, they are powerful aids in mobilizing every human being's innate abilities to heal and balance themselves.

The Heartbeat

It is no coincidence that your heart races when you are upset and slows down when you feel calmer. Besides the physical requirements of getting more blood to the vital organs faster, the sound and feel of a heart beating fast speeds up our reactions and helps to create a sense of urgency.

A racing heart in positive situations, such as being in love, also prepares us for action.

Musicians have known and used this fact through the ages to create specific emotions and experiences with their music. Even without a melody, the varying tempi in a shaman's drumming are crucial to the start, development, and call-back from a shamanic journey.

It is not only events but also decision-taking, that can lead to much stress and upset. Sometimes the importance of a decision gets so overwhelming that we can't think straight anymore and feelings of depression are not uncommon.

Allow your heart to take the lead. Open your mind to its guidance; invite it to soothe your emotions and give you a clear mind.

Let's do an easy meditation exercise together to help you get more in touch with your heart.

Sit or lie down in a comfortable place, where you'll be undisturbed for about 20 minutes.

Close your eyes if you feel comfortable doing that or fix a soft, unfocused gaze somewhere ahead.

Breathe in deeply from your stomach without lifting your shoulders, hold your breath for a moment or two, and exhale fully. Visualize blowing out all the feelings of stress on your breath and see them leave you.

Try to keep your mind neutral but don't force anything—you do not have to stop thinking. See the thoughts coming and going like fish swimming past in an aquarium.

Breathe in again and visualize the breath going into your heart, opening it up. Breathe out again.

Put one hand over your heart now and breathe into your heart again. Hold the thought in your mind that you are touching something sacred, given to you by the universe. Hold the breath in your heart for a moment before releasing it fully.

Still holding your hand gently over your heart, breathe in again and send the gentlest of hugs to your heart on your breath. Feel warm gratitude for the power of your heart flooding your being. Breathe out again.

Keep breathing in...caressing and thanking your heart...and breathing out again for as long as you want.

When you feel ready, open your eyes and move your body.

Keep that open, loving feeling in and around you when you go on with your day. Give your brain a break if it has been doing all the hard work lately. Leave the doubts, second-guessing, and limiting beliefs behind and move to the song of your heart. Your gut feeling actually lives in your heart.

Breathing and Sighs

Every inhalation brings life force to our existence. With every sigh and exhalation, we have the opportunity to get rid of everything that opposes our life force and makes our existence difficult.

Since ancient times, people have viewed breathing as an equivalent to life. One of the best examples of this is the Egyptian *Books of Breathing*, dating back to about 350 BCE. They were texts intended to teach people how to continue living in the afterlife. The first chapter starts with these words: "Do not show this script to anybody. It may benefit only the shades who, confined to the Underworld, are reborn endlessly in the breath of truth" (Balsamo & Dagnese, 2012).

A scientific study in Australia to assess the physiological impact of slow, deep breathing found that feeling better when breathing consciously is not only all in the mind. The scientists found that controlled slow breathing changes the parameters of bodily systems that influence health and longevity, significantly. The systems include heart rate, the strength of the respiratory muscles, and the efficiency of oxygen exchange. They also found slow breathing toned the vagus nerve. The vagus nerve stimulates the parasympathetic nervous system and that, in turn, sends signals to the body to relax and calm down (Russo et al., 2017).

In our hectic modern lifestyles, we have forgotten how powerful breathing can be. Taking deep, controlled breaths is the last thing on our minds when we have to take care of a stressful job, family responsibilities, and health and environmental challenges.

Take a moment to become aware of your breathing and use your sighs as vehicles to get rid of the tension stored in your body.

Incorporate sound in your deep breathing by doing an exercise that is called the lion's breath (simhasana) in Sanskrit.

Sit comfortably and lean forward slightly, supporting your hands on your knees.

Keep your fingers spread as widely as possible without putting stress on your fingers or hands.

Inhale deeply through your nose.

Now open your mouth widely and stick your tongue out, stretching it down toward your chin.

Exhale forcefully, feeling the breath move over the back of your tongue, and making a deep 'haaa' sound.

Be aware of the vibrations the sound sends through your body and welcome them.

Breathe normally a couple of times.

Repeat the lion's breath six or seven times.

A quieter breath-sound exercise that will also allow you to experience powerful calming vibrations is known as the humming bee breath.

Sit comfortably with your eyes closed or your unfocused gaze fixed somewhere ahead.

Keep your back straight.

Close your ears with your index or middle fingers.

Keep your mouth closed but leave a slight opening between your upper and lower teeth.

Breathe deeply through your nose without moving your shoulders, allowing your abdomen to expand.

Exhale while making a smooth, humming sound like a bee. The sound need not be loud.

Continue breathing this way for about five minutes, keeping full awareness of the vibrations throughout your body.

If any thoughts pop up during this time, put them aside gently for later. Try to remember them after the exercise—they might be answers you've been seeking for a long time.

A Meditation to Unify the Heart and the Breath

Try this effective but simple meditation to combine your heart and breathing into a powerful inner symphony to calm and heal you. Do it once a day for a month and see if you experience any benefits from it.

It involves three deep breaths.

Stand comfortably with your feet spread slightly wider than your shoulders, as if your body is in the form of a pyramid.

Place your hands gently over your heart.

Inhale deeply and calmly while visualizing the breath coming in through your feet, moving up through your legs, hips, abdomen, and chest, reaching your heart.

Exhale with a forceful sigh. Imagine expelling the breath from your heart, taking with it all the stagnant energy that was trapped in your lower body.

Visualize your feet safely and firmly connected to the earth.

For the second breath, extend your arms fully above your head. Imagine your body forming an upside-down pyramid that points at your heart.

Breathe in again and while you listen to the sound of your breath, visualize it coming in through the top of your head, moving down through your brain, face, neck, shoulders, upper back, and chest, and reaching your heart.

Exhale again forcefully while imagining expelling stagnant energy on the breath from your upper body as well as your mind.

Visualize an open communication channel to the divine energy of the cosmos, stretching through your arms upward.

The third breath will balance the earth and sky energies in the heart.

Lower your arms and place your hands again over your heart.

Inhale audibly and deeply through your nose and visualize the breath entering your heart.

Exhale forcefully and visualize the breath going out from your heart again.

Stand quietly for a moment and savor the quiet, calm feeling of connectedness.

Take this feeling with you wherever you go for the rest of the day.

EARTH'S OWN MUSIC

Did you know the earth has a song, vibrating at its own frequency? It is known as the Schumann resonances. You can tap into it too and use its healing properties to enhance your life.

In 1952, the German scientist Winfried Otto Schumann, who was a professor at the Technische Hochschule in München, suggested the existence of low-frequency resonances in the cavity formed between the earth's surface and the ionosphere. The ionosphere is the very top part of the earth's atmosphere that borders space, stretching from 50 to 400 miles above the earth (Besser, 2007).

The Schumann resonances are electromagnetic frequencies in the extremely low range of 7 to 8 Hz. The electromagnetic waves are put into motion by lightning strikes all over the planet that happen many times per second.

These frequencies also resonate with 432 Hz.

MUSIC THERAPY

We are more than physical bodies. We have mental, spiritual, and emotional bodies too. All these facets that make up a human being have to synchronize in tempo and musical key, otherwise, the music that emanates from us is fragmented and dissonant.

Emotions act as the conductor of the orchestra and when they are upset, everything tends to get into a shambles.

When our emotions are positive, on the other hand, scientific research has proven all our systems run smoothly (McCraty et al., 1995).

This dynamic interaction is known in biology as coherence.

The right music can play an essential role in obtaining coherence in the body when we allow ourselves to adapt to its constant rhythm. That is called entrainment.

An interesting article published in the Journal of Music Therapy noted that even the sound of a metronome at a steady, relaxing 66 beats per minute reduced anxiety more effectively than sitting in silence (Gadberry, 2011).

Our emotions also vibrate. Negative emotions such as anger and resentment vibrate at a lower frequency than positive feelings. Listening to the right music can lift the vibration of negative emotions and thereby influence our emotional well-being.

Anxiety and Depression

Music therapy and other forms of sound healing have been effective in helping sufferers of anxiety, panic attacks, and depression. Even when only used in conjunction with conventional forms of therapy, studies have found higher success rates with those people who received the musical component too (Erkkilä et al., 2011).

The brain processes the rhythm, tempo, and pitch in separate locations and when all of these combine in a calming experience, it can change a person's life for the better.

Except for meditations, there usually are no verbal components to this therapy in the same sense that conversations have to take place with other types of therapists. This makes the effect of music therapy that much stronger, being targeted at a part of our emotional and mental makeup that has existed before speech. Linear, logical patterns and cognitive reasoning cannot interfere with calming anxiety and lifting depression on a subconscious level.

On a physiological level, doing an enjoyable activity causes the brain to release the hormone dopamine that is known as the "pleasure hormone," as well as endorphins, also known as the "feel-good hormones," that are chemical components capable of reducing stress.

Anxious reactions to outside stimuli occur when our fight-or-flight response gets activated. While ancient man had to contend with real tigers and lions chasing them, our modern society has symbolic wild animals baying for our blood such as hectic work schedules, deadlines, and a never-ending stream of text and email messages. Often these stress factors are ongoing—they won't let themselves be killed like physical tigers. We never get to turn off the adrenaline and cortisol rush of fight-or-flight and it has negative consequences for our emotions and bodies.

Calming down the nervous inner chatter helps us to settle the stress responses too. Music works on the parasympathetic nervous system of the body, which is the network that allows us to feel safe, settled, and supported.

When the parasympathetic system is activated, the sympathetic network stops producing the inflammation-inducing hormone cortisol and adrenaline production decreases rapidly.

If the music vibrates at a frequency that is especially beneficial to our emotions, a quiet and calm sympathetic nervous network opens the way for our bodies to take on the healing frequency and find their own inner harmony again.

A Healing Meditation For Depression

Play your choice of soothing music or soundscape in the background while doing this guided meditation.

If you want to listen to solfeggio frequencies, 741 Hz is the one that facilitates change and helps us find our inner, true voice again. An alternative is the universal frequency of 528 Hz.

Settle down in a comfortable position and close your eyes if you are comfortable doing so. If not, you can direct an unfocused, soft gaze to the floor.

Be gentle with yourself and listen to the needs of your body. If it needs to lie down, do so. If your body wants you to sit, perhaps in a favorite armchair, honor its request.

Become aware of the feeling of your feet on the floor or your legs touching the fabric of the chair. Allow this sensation to assure you that you are grounded and safe on a solid surface.

Place one of your hands over your heart and position the other one over your lower belly.

Inhale deeply through your nose, feeling your belly rising as you pull the life-giving breath entering and filling you.

Slowly exhale completely, feeling your belly flattening again.

And breathe in again deeply into your belly...and out completely.

Be conscious of the air nourishing every muscle and every cell in your body, moving through you and bringing new life.

And breathe in again deeply into your belly...and out completely. Imagine the exhaled breath carrying away any heaviness and sadness from every corner of your being.

Become aware of a sensation of lightness in your body.

Continue breathing this way for a minute or two, focusing on the rhythm of your breathing and your feeling of freedom and lightness only.

[Pause]

Getting distracted is also okay, be gentle with yourself. Just return your attention to your breathing.

Feel yourself opening up to make space for gratitude and feeling easy after the heaviness has left.

[Pause]

Look at yourself with compassion and recognize the heavy burden you have been carrying, living with depression. Assure yourself that you understand why you feel depleted and used up and hug yourself mentally for staying strong for so long.

Give yourself the time and kindness that your struggle with depression deserves.

If your inner voice comes up with judgment and accusations, breathe compassion and love into it and see it dissolve on your exhaled breath.

Become aware of the easy stillness that has come into the core of your being and savor its presence.

Allow yourself to hope again for a better today, a better tomorrow, a better life.

Breathe in again deeply into your belly...and out completely.

Feel the breath moving through your body and fill you from your toes up to the crown of your head.

Remembering the easy stillness, open your eyes when you are ready.

BINAURAL BEATS

Another popular concept in New Age terminology is binaural beats. Some people believe in their effectiveness firmly, while others reject the claims as hype for nothing.

They can be a great aid in sound healing, however. Let's look at what binaural beats really are and how they work.

What Are Binaural Beats and How Do They Work?

One way to describe the phenomenon would be to think of it as an auditory brain illusion with real effects. It is a beat created entirely by the brain.

Binaural beats only work when listening through stereo headphones. A tone at one frequency is played in one ear and a tone with a slightly different frequency is played in the other ear, at the same time. The sounds arrive independently at the inferior colliculus in the midbrain, which is where auditory input is processed. The brain combines the two different tones into a new frequency that creates a pulsing effect, which is perceived as one incoming sound. The sound that is heard does not actually exist.

It is easy to test whether you are hearing binaural beats or regular, acoustic beats. If you lift one stereo headphone from your ear, you will hear only one tone playing in the other ear. The same is true for the other side if you reverse the process. If you replace both earphones, the pulsing beat will be back. That is proof that the frequencies are 'mixed' by your brain and not by the speakers before the sounds reach your ears.

The frequencies are chosen to align with the frequencies of the five states of brain waves. The brain aligns itself with the combined frequency it hears, in what is known as the frequency-following effect.

It is therefore possible to induce a specific brain wave frequency in the brain by listening to binaural beats at the right frequency. This is what is meant by brain entrainment—you draw your brain into a desired and chosen mental state.

- Brain entrainment can work negatively, for example in people with epilepsy. Seizures can be triggered by flashing lights or certain rhythms in music that entrain the brain to a frequency where it malfunctions in terms of that specific person's physical makeup.

The brain waves involved are the five main states discussed earlier in this chapter. Just to recap, they are, from slowest to fastest:

- Delta: Deep sleep, healing, intense meditation, and accessing the subconscious.
- Theta: Meditation, relaxation, and creative activities.
- Alpha: Focus, learning activities, positive thoughts, and relaxation.
- Beta: Sharply focused, solving problems, analytical thinking, and energetic.
- Gamma: Advanced cognitive action, great attention to detail, and unorthodox creativity.

The biggest test for any type of treatment or intervention remains whether it really works. Medical opinions are divided about their effectiveness but research is ongoing.

Sound therapists and healers have been using them successfully for many years to alleviate anxiety and combat depression.

It is worth noting that some studies found binaural beats in the lower frequencies (theta and delta) increased depression, while those in the higher frequencies, such as beta, consistently lowered anxiety levels and decreased depression.

The same holds true for memory enhancement or hindering. Higher frequencies produced better memory recall, while slower frequencies interfered with it (Chaieb et al., 2015).

It is important to remember that humans are very different from each other, despite our similarities. Experiment with binaural beats until you find the one that works for the purpose you need it for.

Important Things to Remember

When starting out with binaural beats, it can be tempting to overdo it to speed up results. It will, however, not work that way.

- Start with the slower frequencies rather than the quick ones to give your brain a chance to adapt to the new pattern.

- Listen through the whole track from start to finish. Don't jump into it in the middle, thinking you'll get to the powerful stuff quicker. The tracks are designed to work up to a climax and back down again. It is a bit like warming up first in the gym before starting your exercise routine.
- Limit listening time to 90 minutes per day for the first two weeks. Just like your muscles, the brain also needs time to rest between entrainment exercises.
- Don't turn the volume up too high. The brain focuses better on the sound if the volume is low. You should just be able to hear the wobbling sound of the beat.
- Some people experience side-effects from binaural beats at the beginning such as slight nausea, headaches, and old memories and emotions resurfacing. This is natural because you are building new neural pathways in your brain and rearranging, so to speak, some things. It will pass after a few days. Once the new pathway is formed, it will be there for you to access when you need it to change your brain wave state.

There are many binaural beat soundtracks available for a free download if you want to experiment first before spending money to purchase tracks.

Keep the above guidelines in mind and start using them to your advantage.

ASMR

Another useful technique is autonomous sensory meridian response (ASMR).

It can be explained as a pleasant tingling sensation on the scalp, neck, upper spine, and sometimes the legs, that is produced by auditory stimuli. It helps people to feel more alert while remaining relaxed and deeply calm.

The stimuli can include anything from whispers, light tapping, brush strokes, and towels being folded, to loud chewing, light patterns, and playing with artificial slime.

The name autonomous sensory meridian response was coined in 2010 by Jennifer Allen. Discussions about the phenomenon started in 2007 on a Facebook group but at that point, no one knew what to call the feelings or what caused them. Some people gave sexual content to the sensations, likening the brain tingles to an orgasm, although most people seem to agree that it has nothing to do with sexual arousal.

Allen proposed the now-accepted name to standardize the terminology and keep it neutral.

The Effects of ASMR

According to neuroscientific investigations, there are definite physiological responses when listening to these auditory inputs.

In an online interview, psychologist and neuroscientist Nick Davis from Manchester explained that the heart rate slows and the hairs on the skin stand on end. This is induced by the associated psychological state that the sounds trigger for the listener. Davis proposes that the sounds bring up sensations of being safe, warm, and comforted because the sounds are soft enough that you would normally only hear them if you were very close to someone (Wired, 2019).

In a study where participants watched ASMR videos in an fMRI scanner, their brains showed activity in the areas where emotions, behaviors associated with pleasing people, and empathy were located. The activities in these brain regions were previously observed by scientists when study participants listened to exceptionally moving music that caused the phenomenon known as *frisson*, as well as during social bonding experiences (Lochte et al., 2018).

The question can be asked whether the noisy and intimidating environment of an fMRI machine could have been inhibiting to the participants. If yes, it implies that even more brain regions could be involved that we don't know of yet.

How Is ASMR Relevant to Sound Healing?

One of the emotional symptoms commonly experienced by patients of sound healers is a feeling of isolation, often accompanied by anxiety and depression. Our modern lifestyles and the abundance of online communication are not conducive to the same degree of social contact and bonding earlier generations knew.

If the theory that one of the possible roots for ASMR lies in the grooming behavior of animals is accepted, it is easy to see how the ASMR sounds that stimulate a feeling of closeness can help someone overcome thoughts of being lonely and anxious.

The detailed nature of some of the ASMR videos also points to watchers of the videos experiencing a feeling of being paid attention to by someone close to them. The sounds are reassuring.

Psychologist Nick Davis has suggested the possibility of an affinity for ASMR stimulation being a genetic trait. Depression and other mental conditions can also have a genetic component—maybe that is not coincidental (Wired, 2019).

The same sounds that bring comfort to lovers of ASMR can bring immense irritation and an intense aversion to others. This condition is known as misophonia and is also often genetic.

Many of the people who become aficionados of ASMR videos and activities have a caring, emotionally vulnerable, and empathetic disposition in common, according to some scientists. They might be more open to allowing responses to external stimuli to come through in their conscious world than those with a different emotional framework (Wired, 2019).

If you look at the comments on the ASMR videos posted on sites like YouTube, it becomes clear that people experience real relief from conditions such as insomnia, mood swings, and loneliness.

ISOCHRONIC TONES

Another tool at the disposal of brain entrainment creators is the technique of using isochronic tones.

They are short, singular tones that come and go at regular intervals and can be used alongside binaural and monaural beats. They create sharp, distinctive sounds and are often embedded in nature sounds.

Isochronic tones are used, together with the other types of brain entrainment techniques, to treat insomnia, anxiety, pain management, mood regulation, and attention deficit hyperactivity disorder (ADHD).

Far less research has been done on isochronic tones than on monaural and binaural beats.

SUBLIMINAL MESSAGE-INFUSED PASSIVE HEALING

Subliminal messages are information given to the brain in such a short time frame that it is not registered consciously. It falls below what is known as the absolute threshold level of our conscious awareness. Even if we look for these messages, we would not be able to detect them. This includes auditory, sensory, and visible stimuli.

This must be seen in contrast with supraliminal messages that can be detected, we just don't necessarily notice them.

The popular story about the origins of subliminal messaging started in 1957 with a marketing researcher named James Vicary. He claimed to have boosted the sales of Coca-Cola and popcorn during the screening of the Academy Award-winning film *Picnic* by flashing very short ads for the two products on the screen every five seconds. The ads were only 1/3,000th of a second long.

In a follow-up experiment, Vicary could not replicate these results and later admitted to lying about the whole thing.

Subsequent research found that subliminal messages can work but they cannot force anyone to do or buy something against their will. They only work when there is an existing desire.

When used in healing techniques, subliminal messaging can strengthen the patient's intention to get better because the desire is already there—the person wants to feel better and calmer.

In a study done in England, psychologists proved that depressed people are tuned to subconscious signals and information that will reinforce their negative mental state. The people don't know they're doing it and cannot consciously stop it or change their behavior (Mogg et al., 1993).

A sound healer can tap into this subconscious behavior and

counter the negative messages with positive statements and encouragement, coaxing the person's subconscious to start looking for positive reinforcement rather than depressing statements and information.

How To Make Your Own Subliminal Messages

Hearing subliminal messages tailored to your needs and delivered in your own voice can be much more powerful than purchasing something made by a stranger.

You don't need complicated computer software or engineering-level skills to do it either.

Download any of the free audio editors available, such as Audacity, that is simple to use and user-friendly to learn. Make sure you have a working microphone that plugs directly into your computer to get clear recordings, such as the microphones that form part of a headset.

Make a list of exactly what you want to say. Formulate your subliminals to the last word so you can just read and put your emotion into it when it's time to record, without having to think about the content.

Be specific. "I want to be depression-free in 90 days" is more focused on the present and what you want to achieve than "I want to be happy."

Keep your messages positive. Don't concentrate on what you don't want but rather on what you do want as a replacement for the undesired situation. "I don't want to be depressed anymore" puts the focus on the negative side of your life. Rather use "I am not depressed anymore"—start from a perspective as if you have achieved your goal already.

Use present tense and write from your heart. You know your true desires better than anyone else.

Record your messages with your chosen music and export the file to a format that can play on your phone or computer such as mp3.

ॐ 7 ॐ

TUNE YOUR BODY, MIND, AND SOUL INTO AN UPGRADED PARADIGM

L istening to a musical instrument that is out of tune grates on the mind and feelings. It just doesn't sit right, even if you're not a musical guru and can't pinpoint the problem. You just know you are uneasy and something has to change.

The same situation happens in our bodies, minds, and souls when our inner melodies go out of tune. We get distressed and uneasy, often without knowing why. The distress can show itself in disease in the body and mind.

Sound healing can retune our harmonies to function together again into the glorious symphony we were created to be.

RECOVERY AND TOTAL WELLNESS THROUGH SOUND

Great progress has been made in the fields of vibrational and regenerative medicine over the last decades. This proves, even to the skeptics, that our bodies are made up of vibrations and energy. Sound waves are an integral part of manipulating and resetting our vibrations to obtain optimum wellness.

The scientist Nikola Tesla said all the secrets of the universe can be found if you think in terms of energy, frequency, and vibration.

Health is mostly about the degree of homeostasis we can achieve among all these factors. A healthy person vibrates, as a whole, at a constant tempo and all the cells and organs are in tune with each other.

Any upset to this uniform, stable tempo of vibration causes disease and discomfort. Bringing our energy and vibrations back to where they should be through the use of tools such as tuning forks and singing bowls is an excellent and non-invasive way to regain total wellness.

Vibrational Movement

While some vibrations consist of big waves we can see, such as ocean tides and changing seasons, there are vibrations on every scale happening in and around us all the time.

Under powerful atomic microscopes, scientists detected nano vibrations, even smaller than 1/1,000th of the diameter of a human hair. Every nano vibration generates an electromagnetic field that influences the chemical composition responsible for the functioning of our cells. The same type of energy has been detected emitting from the hands of Reiki and Qigong practitioners (Kučera & Havelka, 2012).

Different molecules vibrate at different rates and when there is a change in the vibrational environment, it will influence all the molecules. The influence can sometimes be for the worse.

Our behavior, thoughts, ambient temperature, and environment are some of the factors that can change the vibrational tempo in cells and molecules down to the nano level. Music can do the same thing, as shown in previous chapters.

A healthy system of vibrational energy is vital for physical, mental, and spiritual health.

The right sounds at the right frequencies, combined with breathing exercises, meditation, yoga, a responsible physical exercise program, a healthy diet, and healing touch modalities such as Reiki will be a winning formula to get yourself back on track to attain full health in all aspects.

Later in this chapter, we'll look in more detail than previously discussed at some of the tools available to practice sound healing.

Energy Medicine

One of the fields in complementary therapy is called energy medicine. While it includes some of the touch therapies, it is a wide concept that touches on regenerative medicine as well. Regenerative medicine is concerned with techniques to repair and replace diseased and dysfunctional tissues, cells, and organs.

The basis for energy medicine lies in quantum physics and Einstein's demonstration that energy and matter are interchangeable. No matter exists with complete certainty but rather only with the possibility to exist. That means we can change the condition of matter with the addition of specific types and amounts of energy.

This principle has been in use in orthopedics to heal bone breaks where the bone failed to heal through conventional methods. This is known as a chronic nonunion fracture. Through the use of a pulsed electromagnetic field induced by specialized equipment, the same type of current is induced in a broken bone that mechanical manipulation would have produced. That helps the fracture to heal (Prestwood, 2003).

ESSENCE AND ENERGETIC RE-CREATION

We are constantly bombarded with discordant disharmonious frequencies. Anxious or angry interactions with people, stress, noisy or polluted environments, feelings of guilt, and sadness are only a few of the sound challenges we face every day.

All of these things pull our systems out of tune and when the disrupted condition continues long enough, we start suffering from illness in mind and body. Practitioners of energy medicine believe the changes in our cells caused by disharmony open the gates for bacteria and viruses to enter and flourish.

Human beings consist of much more than just the sum of our physical components—we are not a machine like earlier scientists thought. We are made up of several subtle energy bodies too, that form the whole of our being. The interaction between our energy bodies and our physical form creates our existence on earth.

The energies can be knocked out of balance easily and rebalancing is essential to stay true to our essence.

There are seven energy bodies, also called biofields, that have been recognized since early times. They are the etheric, emotional, lower mental, higher mental, causal, soul, and integrated spiritual bodies.

- The etheric body is the closest to the physical body. It is denser than any of the other bodies. It contains the energy 'master plan' of the physical body and vibrates at a slightly higher frequency than the physical.
- The emotional body is the home of our feelings and emotions.
- The lower mental body accommodates our mental processes and rational thoughts. Thoughts driven by a specific emotion can take on a material form.
- The higher mental body receives insights from the spiritual realm.
- The causal body is the doorway to the collective consciousness of all humankind.
- The soul body is pure spirit. Inspiration and information needed by the lower bodies are obtained here and filtered through to where they are needed.
- The integrated spiritual body merges all the other subtle bodies.

The lines of energy that run through all of our bodies are known by different names. The Indian Ayurvedic literature talks about nadis, while TCM calls them meridians.

The channels run through seven energy vortices that connect them, known as chakras. Chakras are depicted as spinning wheels of energy that can be thrown off balance or blocked, resulting in off-kilter energy running at the wrong vibrational tempo.

Although some ancient literature speaks of 112 chakras, there are seven that are generally recognized. It is worth outlining the chakras once again, as they are of significant importance.

The chakras are arranged through the body from low to high.

- The root chakra: Located at the base of the spine, the root chakra is the seat of our physical connection to the earth, feelings of mental stability, self-confidence, and the degree to which we feel safe and secure. It is associated with the legs and feet.
- The sacral chakra: Just above the root chakra, in the middle of the lower abdomen, and about four fingers below the navel, is the second chakra. It is connected to reproductive health, as well as the emotional side of relationships.
- The solar plexus chakra: It is situated in the area of the navel and is believed to be a meeting point for all the nadis, or energy channels, that run through the body. It is associated with self-image and digestive issues.
- The heart chakra: It is found where the physical heart is and relates to all things regarding love for the self and others.
- The throat chakra: It is at the base of the throat and rules all types of communication, the confidence to speak out for the truth, as well as the head, neck, shoulders, and mouth.
- The third eye chakra: This is located between the eyebrows and in the center of the head. It relates to the connection of the self to the spiritual world and enhances intuition.
- The crown chakra: The seventh chakra is located outside the body, at the crown of the head. It is described as a bridge between heaven and earth. Physically, the crown chakra is associated with coordination and the neurological system.

DEEP RELAXATION AND WHOLENESS

The best reset switch for our bodies and minds is deep relaxation. It turns off harmful chemical reactions, strengthens the immune system, and brings peace to our hearts.

Sound is one of the most effective ways to relax fully. A sound bath can cleanse you down to a cellular level, the way a physical soak in the tub can do for your body. The harmonic vibrations stimulate alpha and theta brain waves that make deep healing possible. The heart rate and respiratory system slow down, the blood pressure drops to relaxed levels, and stress can be released completely.

People with chronic illnesses and pain can benefit greatly from regular sound baths.

The sound is less structured than conventional music, allowing the mind to roam free of preoccupations with rhythms and melody.

Singing bowls, chimes, and gongs are some of the instruments commonly used. They will be discussed in more detail later.

The effects of a sound bath are similar to those experienced with regular deep meditation.

A study undertaken by German and Austrian scientists on the effectiveness of music added to a relaxation program found definite better results among the group who listened to music too (Kappert et al., 2019).

A NEW PARADIGM OF HOLISTIC MEDICINE

The Western scientific and medical approach has always been reductionist, in contrast to the Eastern model of a holistic paradigm.

According to reductionist principles, a whole is broken down into its constituent parts to understand how the whole works. It is accepted that the whole cannot be more than the sum of its parts.

Nerves, blood cells, bones, and muscles must provide all the answers to medical questions and facilitate all cures.

A patient is often looked at in isolation from his/her history and environment because they are viewed as subjective factors that can't be taken into account.

A procedure performed in a certain way and within certain parameters is expected to deliver the same results every time. Any deviations are viewed unfavorably.

Practitioners' worldview is often one of a chaotic universe that can only be managed through dissection and control.

In contrast to this, a holistic attitude starts from the belief that the whole can never be understood by looking at its parts only because it is much bigger than its visible parts.

Memories of the past, together with the present environment, are seen as interacting partners regarding the patient's health.

The practitioner's senses are just as much a part of the diagnosing procedure as any medical equipment.

Opposite outcomes in procedures are taken in stride because it is accepted that humans differ greatly, especially when viewed within the framework of their past.

Remedies are used just as nature created them.

To holistic health practitioners, the universe is an ordered, organic, and meaningful place to be studied and enjoyed.

Sound healing strives to be fully holistic to heal the entire person, not just one organ.

EXPLORING THE INNER-DIMENSIONAL SOUND CHAMBER

The cells in the body were made to regenerate themselves according to complex geometric patterns.

Assisting with this is a device created by acupressurist and Reiki master Tom Hunt, that he calls the inner-dimensional sound chamber. According to online resources, only a few of the chambers are in operation across America but those who have been treated in them, have found the experience to be remarkably relaxing and balancing (Sound Coherence, n.d.).

The structure has a hollow framework built in a sacred geometrical pattern that is said to resemble the gridlike frame around the cosmos. Specialized music is played through the structure, creating vibrational patterns that move molecules on their most basic level to heal and relax the body.

Hunt believes an hour of sound meditation in his chamber is equivalent to a year's worth of deep meditation (Sound Coherence, n.d.).

SOUND SYNTHESIS

Sound synthesis is the process of creating a sound signal electronically, without the presence of any type of acoustic source.

This has given rise to what has become known as electronic meditation. Sounds produced by a synthesizer can be played through speakers that can be embedded in recliners or massage tables, to provide an immersion in vibration and sound. Techniques such as binaural beats all make use of this technology.

Another type of electronic sound healing is called bioacoustics therapy. It involves analyzing someone's voice for so-called missing frequencies. Proponents of the therapy say the missing frequencies are related to illnesses in the body and mind. They produce a recording of those frequencies and the patient listens to the recording regularly until the vocal profile is complete.

In cymatic therapy, organs are exposed to specific frequencies and combinations of frequencies that have been carefully selected to balance and heal that organ (Snow, 2011).

Some people do not agree that electronic signals can deliver the same effective healing as acoustic sounds, while others believe using more electronic equipment will make the therapies more agreeable to the mainstream medical community.

SOUND BALANCING WITH TUNING FORKS

When disease alerts you to the fact that your body has gone out of its rhythm, a tuning session with tuning forks could be all you need. The tuning forks stimulate the body to start its natural healing process and strengthen the immune system to assist with this.

Through vibrations traveling throughout the body carried in the water which makes up the biggest part of our bodies, tuning forks open the energy pathways, help to remove blockages, relieve pain, and release tension.

What Are Tuning Forks?

Tuning forks are resonating devices, meaning they can produce a sound, and they are usually made of aluminum. In earlier times, steel was used. They consist of two prongs, or tines, in a U-shape that sit on top of a handle, or stem.

Tuning forks were invented in 1711 by a British musician called John Shore to tune musical instruments.

The pitch of the musical note they emit when the prongs are hit against the heel of the palm or an object is determined by the length and mass of the prongs. The device is held by the stem because the two prongs of the fork shape vibrate in opposite directions and touching the stem does not affect its movement at all.

Tuning forks produce a pure tone. The harmonic overtone that is automatically created when the prongs are struck to start the fundamental tone dies out quickly because of the forked design, and the fundamental tone is sustained on its own for quite a while. That makes it an effective tool for sound healers.

They are manufactured to deliver frequencies from 64 Hz to 4,096 Hz and are usually sold in sets covering all the frequencies. They don't need attention too often to stay on pitch.

Some tuning forks have a round weight at the tops of each prong. The weights can slide up and down. They are called weighted tuning forks or Otto tuners. The word 'Otto' is short for 'osteophonic.' 'Osteo' relates to bones and 'phonic' to sound.

The weights can strengthen the vibration delivered so it can reach the bones to ease joint pain.

What Are Tuning Forks Used For?

Sound healing practitioners use tuning forks to relieve tension, ease muscle and joint pain, reduce inflammation by stimulating the release of nitric oxide into the bloodstream, ease muscle spasms, calm anxiety, center, ground, rebalance body systems to bring homeostasis, boost digestion, and promote deep sleep.

The vibrations work on energy channels and points in a somewhat similar way to acupuncture, only using sound instead of needles to stimulate the body.

Important Points When Shopping For Tuning Forks

There are many different types available and choosing a fork or set can be difficult. Which metal should it be made from, weighted or unweighted, which frequencies are the best...especially in the beginning the options can be confusing.

The first question to answer is what you want to use the tuning forks for. What are your intentions and needs? Do you want to use them in a healing practice or just for yourself? Are you still experimenting with their effects or are you experienced in their use? What types of ailments and problems will you be treating?

It is also important to approach your choice with your gut feel too, not only with left-brained reasoning. Some tuning forks will resonate with your soul without making a sound and others will not. Ultimately, your decision should be based on who you are as well as on what you want to do.

Some sets are based on solfeggio frequencies with their roots in numerology and the digits three, six, and nine. Solar harmonic sets are based on the five elements of water, fire, earth, ether, and air. Which set are you drawn to?

Close your eyes and think of each of the sets you are considering. Do you feel any unease when thinking about one of them? Then the other one is probably the one you should choose.

Solfeggio Tuning Forks

The solfeggio musical scale is part of a system believed to be old, even older than the well-known Gregorian chants that utilize them. They are also reputed to have been used in ancient Indian Sanskrit teachings and ceremonies.

Each tone comprises frequencies that are believed to impart blessings and spiritual balance to anyone listening to them.

The name solfeggio comes from the use of sol-fa syllables to denote the tones—a musical system known as solmization. Originally there were six frequencies. Three more were added later. The syllables for the first six are ut, re, mi, fa, sol, and la.

- **Ut** queant laxis: Liberating guilt and fear
- **Re**sonare fibris: Undoing situations and facilitating change
- **Mi**ra gestorum: Transformation and miracles
- **Fa**muli tuorum: Connecting/relationships
- **Sol**ve polluti: Awakening intuition
- **La**bii reatum: Returning to spiritual order

The six phrases now associated with the solfeggio tones formed most of the first verse of a hymn in honor of John the Baptist, written by Guido of Arezza. Guido used the well-known hymn to teach his music students the sounds and notes of the scale—a scale that was already in existence. The hymn has led many to believe, mistakenly, that Guido was the originator of the solfeggio tones.

The knowledge of solfeggio tones was brought into modern awareness in the 1970s by the researcher and physicist Dr. Joseph Puleo. He used numerological principles to identify the first six frequencies.

They have been called the only pure tones because they are in harmony with the structure of the universe. They are also closely aligned with the Schumann resonances' frequency of 8 Hz (see the discussion of these resonances in chapter 6).

The original frequencies are 396 Hz, 417 Hz, 528 Hz, 639 Hz, 741 Hz, and 852 Hz. The three that were added later are 174 Hz, 285 Hz, and 963 Hz. Solfeggio tuning fork sets usually include all nine frequencies.

174 Hz

It is used to relieve pain and stress. Some healers describe it as a natural anesthetic that brings a sense of being safe and secure to all the organs in the body. It has a low, soothing quality to the sound that is a good start to any grounding and centering session.

285 Hz

This is the frequency that is used to encourage physical rejuvenation to repair damage to cells and tissues. It also targets the energetic field to repair holes in the aura, clear blockages, and align all the chakras.

396 Hz

This frequency is credited with being able to penetrate deep into our subconscious to bring freedom from fear and guilt, and alleviating grief. This will remove any blocks to reaching your full potential.

It is associated with the first, or root, chakra, and the color red.

417 Hz

This frequency brings about positive change and stimulates creativity, helping us to find solutions to problems. It removes negative energy from a person as well as from the environment. It can assist in laying down new, healthier habits.

It can assist in loosening stiff muscles and tight joints to improve mobility.

The frequency is associated with the second, or sacral, chakra, and the color orange.

528 Hz

This frequency is often called the universal frequency of miracles. It is believed to be capable of repairing DNA, transforming relationships, boosting spirituality, and helping a person regain their emotional equilibrium.

It is often used to relieve pain and alleviate anxiety. Many healers use it to help with weight loss because it can form new neural pathways in the brain, leading to healthier eating and lifestyle habits.

It is associated with the third, or solar plexus, chakra, and the color yellow.

639 Hz

This is the frequency of connections. It can help to repair and strengthen relationships between people and with the self, bringing harmony if there was discord. It is also associated with making people brave enough to be emotionally vulnerable, to make intimate connections.

It is associated with the fourth, or heart, chakra, and the color pink.

741 Hz

Also known as the detoxification frequency, 741 Hz helps to purify the body, heart, and mind of harmful intentions and residues. It awakens intuition and boosts mental clarity. It also brings the courage to speak out for one's truth.

It is associated with the fifth, or throat, chakra, and the color blue.

852 Hz

This is the frequency that helps us to align with spiritual truths and regain our awareness of the spiritual order of all things.

It helps us to recognize illusions and see through them. It can bring about deep and meaningful dreams.

The frequency is associated with the sixth, or third eye, chakra, and the color violet/purple.

936 Hz

The highest tone of them all is the one that brings us closer to a perfect state of unity with the spirit of the universe.

It can assist with spiritual channeling and contacting ascended masters and higher dimensions.

It is associated with the seventh, or crown, chakra and the colors white or gold.

Solar Harmonic Tuning Forks

A set of solar harmonic tuning forks consist of a full octave of music notes, starting at C and ending at the next C. Each note has a specific frequency. They are used together to utilize the intervals between the notes.

The C-note (256 Hz) and G-note (384 Hz) together are specifically effective. The interval between them is known as the perfect fifth. They vibrate together at a ratio of 2:3. That means the C-tuning fork vibrates twice as fast as an unstruck C-fork of 128 cycles per second, while the G-tuning fork vibrates three times as fast as that unstruck C.

It is a ratio that is considered sacred in many traditions and is associated with the relationship between mathematics and the universe.

According to some legends, the Greek mathematician Pythagoras considered this interval to be extremely therapeutic and capable of transformation. A set consisting of these two tuning forks only is also known as a Pythagorean set.

The frequencies are, in Hertz:

- 256 (C)
- 288 (D)
- 320 (E)
- 341.3 (F)
- 384 (G)
- 426.7 (A)
- 480 (B)
- 512 (C)

Harmonic tuning forks also work with the five elements of the universe as explained in Ayurvedic teachings. These are space/ether, air, fire, water, and earth.

A person's health and personality depend on the mix of the five elements they have. When one element goes out of balance, the person will not be completely well.

Space/Ether

This is the element of emptiness. It is specifically associated with the mouth, ears, and hearing—cavities that have to be filled by other elements.

Air

Air represents movement, lightness, breathing, and oxygen in Ayurveda. In excess, it can cause hyperactivity. Deficiency in the air element can bring fatigue. Digestive, heart, and joint health are associated with this element.

Fire

Linked to the mind, thoughts, emotions, and obsessions, fire is a powerful Ayurvedic element. Physically, it is linked to the eyes and body temperature.

Water

The element of water is associated with the nervous system, blood supply, joints, saliva, and respiratory system.

Earth

The last element is the grounding one, representing our bones, teeth, nails, and the sense of smell. An overall and inexplicable feeling of weakness in the whole body is also associated with an earth element that is not in harmony with the others.

Fibonacci Tuning Forks

Another way to use the intervals is by working with tuning forks created according to a Fibonacci number sequence.

Their effect when two forks are used together is a spiraling sound that is used to balance the nervous system, increase creativity, heal trauma, and break addictions.

They are sold in sets of eight, starting at the number one. If you already have a harmonic set, it is only necessary to purchase four Fibonacci tuners to have a full set; the two notes of C, the note of G, and the note of A are already part of a harmonic set.

- The interval 1/1 is used to symbolize the beginning of all things, to which everything will return again.
- The interval 1/2 is associated with space. It balances the element of space/ether and helps to cope with loss and grief.
- The interval 2/3 represents balance and works with the nervous system and pituitary gland. It is a good interval to center yourself.
- The interval 3/5 is associated with dreams. In music, it is a sixth interval that is also sometimes called the mystic fire. It helps with the visualization and creation of new ideas.
- The interval 5/8 works with the inner voice. It helps you to access your inner wisdom and peace.

- The interval 8/13 represents the mystical pathway for clean and pure alignment with the source of the universe.
- The interval 13/21 is associated with the great divide between spiritual truths and earthly reality. It assists in establishing communication with higher beings such as angels.
- The interval 21/34 represents the eye of God/god. It relates to the pineal gland and helps us to understand higher realms and see eternal truths in ourselves.

How to Use Tuning Forks to Relieve Pain

Now it is time to get practical. Let's look at three different ways to treat joint and muscle pain, as explained by Jane Satchwell, the Vice-Principal of the Sound Healing Academy in Cornwall, in the United Kingdom (2019).

Using a 174 Hz Unweighted Tuning Fork

In this technique, the tuning fork is not used directly onto the body but just slightly off it.

- Activate the tuning fork by tapping it lightly on a rubber puck or striking it gently with a mallet. The sound will ring clearly and cleanly.
- Hold the ringing tuning fork close to the painful area of the body without actually touching it.
- Reactivate the tuning fork when the sound dies down.
- Keep this up for five to 10 minutes.

Using Either a 128 Hz Tuning Fork or a 136.1 Hz Weighted Tuning Fork

Weighted tuning forks are used directly on the painful area of the body. Their sound is somewhat muted when compared with unweighted tuners.

- Activate the tuning fork.
- Place the lower end of the tuning fork (the stem) on the

muscle or joint that is causing pain. Feel the vibrations of the ringing sound going into your body.

- Reactivate the sound before it dies down completely.
- Keep this up for as long as needed to reduce the discomfort and pain.

Using a Weighted 128 Hz Tuning Fork and a 136.1 Hz Tuning Fork Together

The dissonance created by the pitches of these two tuning forks that are quite close together causes strong vibrations that make it easier to dislodge any stuck energy.

- Activate first the one and then the other tuning fork in close succession so that they ring together.
- Place both on the part of the body to be treated. They should be held close together but not touching.
- Reactivate the vibrations before the sound dies down.
- Keep this up for as long as needed to reduce the discomfort and pain.
- Return to using the first technique for a while longer (using the unweighted 174 Hz tuning fork off the body) if necessary.

Useful Tips

Some painful areas are tender to the touch. Reduce the hardness of the tuning fork by putting a rubber ball on the end of the stem.

You can amplify the vibrations of the tuning fork by placing a crystal at the end of the stem, such as clear quartz that is known as the master healer. Rose quartz is good for emotional release and healing.

Using the Pythagorean Tuning Forks in Cross-Lateralization

The purpose of the process called cross-lateralization is to balance the left and right hemispheres of the brain, using the two tuning forks in the sacred ratio of the fifth interval (a C-note and a G-note together).

- Activate the two tuning forks either simultaneously or in quick succession.
- Holding them by their stems, one in each hand, bring them up to your ears and hold them about two inches away.
- After a few seconds, change your hands around.
- Hold that position for a few seconds and change back to the original position.

How to Use an Otto Weighted Tuning Fork to Treat the Skull

Treating and retuning your skull and brain with a tuning fork will enable you to release tension and heal old emotional wounds.

The Otto 128 Hz weighted tuning fork is specifically for use directly on the bone and the vibrations will be felt through your head and brain.

The skull has two sutures joining the different parts. Treatment works best if the tuning fork is placed along the main suture line called the parietal or sagittal suture, and then on both sides of the line.

- Strike the fork and place it on the front hairline, right in the center of the skull.
- Hold it there during its full cycle.
- When the sound of the tuning fork dies down, strike it again and move your placement point about an inch back from the first one.
- Breathe deeply and calmly and hold the fork still until the vibrations die down.
- Repeat the process twice more, every time moving about an inch back.
- Next, repeat the sequence on four points to the right, and then to the left, of the center suture line.
- Pay attention to any feelings that come up. Be alert to changes in your breathing—do some points make you breathe faster or slower? Those might be bringing up sensations that you have to explore further to heal.

- In the next section, move around both ears in four points, keeping about an inch from the ear.
- Next, move around to the back of the head. Place the tuning fork on points in a triangular shape that has its apex at the top of the head.

A Buyer's Guide

Although tuning forks are generally durable, low-quality alloys can wear out with constant use.

Many of the cheaper versions are molded and their sound quality can be tinny and feeble. Their therapeutic value is not high because their vibrations are not strong.

There are good quality tuning forks made in America that cost a bit more but they are made of a really good alloy that lasts and produces a strong, clear sound.

Look for a supplier that sells good quality hockey pucks to strike them against as a part of the tuning fork set, rather than lightweight wooden sticks that cannot produce a strong sound and will not last long.

A 2021 survey by the Reiki master and regular reviewer of healing equipment, Deborah, from *The Light of Happiness*, listed the top nine brands to consider (The Light of Happiness, 2021b).

- Brand Radical: Therapeutic Chakra Harmonic Planetary 26 Tuning Forks. It consists of a set of eight harmonic tuning forks (an octave), seven chakra balancing tuning forks (tuned to work based on the mathematical rotation of the planets around the sun), and 11 precision tuning forks tuned to the eight planets, Pluto, the sun and moon.

The current price on Amazon (Sep 2021): $299.

- Brand Radical: Chakra and Soul Purpose Cosmic Weighted Healing Tuning Forks with Rubber Balls. The seven weighted tuning forks can each be used directly on the part of the body related to the chakra to be treated. The rubber balls at the ends make it more comfortable on the body.

The current price on Amazon (Sep 2021): $109.

- Brand Radical: Sacred Solfeggio Coloured Tuning Forks. The brightly colored set of six tuning forks are unweighted and should be used around the ears and body.

The current price on Amazon (Sep 2021): $119.

- Brand Omnivos: Solfeggio Tuning Forks. This is another trusted manufacturer and their set of nine tuning forks are made from professional-grade aluminum. The instruments can be used to tune not only the body but also the immediate environment. *The Light of Happiness* has found their forks to be about 26% harder and ring for up to 20% longer than those made by some other manufacturers.

The current price on Amazon (Sep 2021): $149.

- Brand Medivibe: Tuning Forks. The set consists of four forks that produce a pleasing major chord when used together.

The product is currently out of stock and no price could be obtained.

- Brand Radical: 8 Chakra and Soul Weighted Healing Forks. Each fork is related to a chakra. The eighth one relates to the soul purpose chakra.

The current price on Amazon (Sep 2021): $149.

- Brand Tuningforkshop: Nine Chakra Tuning Fork Set.

Besides one fork for each of the seven chakras, the set also includes one for the soul purpose chakra and one for the earth star, or low ohm, chakra.

- Brand Tuningforkshop: Nine Sacred Solfeggio Tuning Forks. The set includes one fork for each solfeggio frequency, a rubber mallet, and a velvet pouch to keep them in.

The current price on Amazon (Sep 2021): $84.

- Brand Kalea: OM Tuning Fork. It is only one weighted tuning fork but it is made to a very high standard, with a bead at the end to make it easier on the body.

The current price on Amazon (Sep 2021): $39.95.

One set to avoid because it is of poor quality, according to the review by *The Light of Happiness*, is Tuningforkshop's 7 Chakra Tuning Fork Set. They found the sound to be tinny and the forks took up to 20 seconds to reach the right frequency. Sometimes the sound did not stabilize at all and that makes these forks unsuitable for healing purposes.

SOUND HEALING WITH SINGING BOWLS AND CRYSTAL BOWLS

The rich tones of singing bowls have been part of healing rituals since ancient times. They are gaining in popularity today but, just as with tuning forks, the choice available if you're looking to purchase bowls can be bewildering.

Some are made of metal, others of crystal; some are decorated and some are plain. There are big bowls, small bowls, deep bowls, and shallow bowls. Each type has its uses and together we'll explore all of them in this section.

How and Why Do Singing Bowls Work?

Singing bowls are also sometimes called Tibetan or Himalayan singing bowls. They have been a part of Tibetan Buddhist rituals for centuries. They started gaining popularity in the Western world with New Age philosophies and many modern yogis and energy medicine practitioners have unwavering faith in their effectiveness.

Traditionally, the bowls were made from different metal alloys including copper, silver, tin, lead, iron, and gold. By the end of the 20th century, crystal bowls became more popular.

When struck gently with a felt or suede-covered striker or mallet, the bowls produce a beautifully clear, ringing sound that is sustained for some time.

When the rim of the bowl is lightly rubbed with the mallet, the friction causes the bowls to produce a high, prolonged whistling sound that is known as their 'singing.' The effect is similar to what you will hear when you rub a wet finger on the edge of a wine glass filled with water. This is called resonance and it is sustained for some time, even after the friction stops. When the bowl is touched with the fingertips, the singing stops.

The volume of the singing is controlled by the tempo at which the edge of the bowl is circled with the mallet.

The ringing sound produces vibrations at the pitch and frequency that largely relate to the size of the singing bowl, although other factors such as the material of which both the bowl and the mallet are made and the surface on which the bowl rests, also play a role.

When the bowl is placed on someone's body or held close to them, the vibrations enter their body and help them to heal, relax, and balance themselves according to the frequency of the sound.

The scientific community is divided in opinion about sound healers' claims regarding the therapeutic effects of singing bowls but anecdotal evidence of their healing and relaxing role abounds.

Some of their reported healing properties include stress relief, deep relaxation, pain relief, muscle regeneration, immune strengthening, blood pressure regulation, relief from depression, and balancing of all the body's energy systems for optimum functioning (Shanti Bowl, n.d.).

In an observational study done by researchers from the University of California to observe the effects of singing bowls on mood, pain relief, and tension release, significant differences were found after the participants completed a meditation with singing bowls. The age group between 40 and 59 seemed to benefit more than the others, especially those people who did not have previous experience with bowls. Their tension levels, as well as physical pain, were much lower, while their spiritual feelings of well-being were measurably higher on a scale of 1 to 5 (Goldsby et al., 2016).

Singing Bowl Frequencies

Assigning a completely accurate frequency reading to a specific bowl can be tricky because many things can influence the pitch of the sound. Striking the sides of the bowl with the mallet will produce a different sound from rubbing the top edge. Striking high on the side-wall will also sound different from a strike low on the side. Rubbing the sidewall also produces a different pitch than rubbing the top.

Singing bowl frequencies can range between 110 Hz and 800 or even 900 Hz. Bowls with bigger diameters generally produce lower frequencies. Thicker walls will bring higher frequencies forth.

The bowls cannot produce chords, only single notes. They can, however, be tuned to a chord such as a fifth interval. Crystal bowls, in contrast to other types of bowls, generally produce a third interval harmonic pattern.

The sounds from metal bowls have three tone colors, so to speak, although it is only one note.

- The fundamental tone is heard when the outside of the sidewall is rubbed with a mallet. It is a slightly lower pitch than the others.
- The highest tone a singing bowl can produce is called its female overtone. That can be heard when the top edge is rubbed with the mallet.
- The third tone color is only present in large to mid-sized bowls. They have a mid-tone that starts once the bowl is warmed up and the female overtone has been played.

The bowls can be tuned to produce specific notes, such as the notes in the harmonic octave, or the solfeggio tones. They can also be made to produce specific octaves.

Differences Between Metal and Crystal Singing Bowls

The sound of crystal bowls is clearer and smoother than that of metal bowls. Crystal bowls don't have the overtones of fundamental, female overtone, and mid-tone. Instead, they produce only one clear, ringing note.

Crystal bowls are not manufactured to specific frequencies like metal bowls. Their size, thickness, and whether they are frosted or not will determine the pitch of their singing. The fast vibration produced by the thick walls of frosted bowls will create a loud sound with a high pitch. A clear bowl of the same size will sound lower and softer.

Adding a Water Dimension

Adding water to your singing bowl meditation can add a great visual and auditory enhancing effect to your relaxation.

The vibrations created in the bowl to produce the sound, get transferred to the water inside the bowl. That sets the water in motion and soon it almost looks as if the water is lightly boiling. In scientific terms, it is known as the Faraday instability of fluids.

The constraints of the bowl change the typical pattern of the Faraday instability enough, however, to cause droplets to start leaping into the air and bouncing on the surface of the water.

The accompanying sound is like light rain falling, which can be very soothing during a meditation. The patterns on the water and any light it might reflect are also mesmerizing.

The general rule is to fill the bowl no more than halfway with the water, to prevent the instability from becoming so great that everything just splashes out.

If you use less than that, there will hardly be anything to see.

It is important to empty the bowl after use and dry it thoroughly to prevent rust and any moldy buildup from forming.

Some people take it a step further and drink the water that was agitated in the singing bowl, or water their plants with it. The belief behind that is that the healing properties of the bowl are transferred to the water.

It is, however, not advisable to drink the water. The bowls are not manufactured to a standard to hold food or drink and elements of the finish and the metals might leak into the water.

Even crystal bowls are not manufactured with the intention to be suitable to hold any food or drink for human consumption and the finish might not be watertight.

Using Singing Bowls in Your Yoga Practice

The restful tones of a singing bowl can bring new depth to your yoga practice. When used at the beginning, it can set the scene for deep relaxation in the body and mind.

It can also be used between positions, or during some positions to promote stillness and mindfulness.

During breathing exercises, a singing bowl can also help to keep the attention focused.

Ending a good yoga session with a singing bowl meditation will settle the harmonic pattern between body and mind and promote deep tranquility.

Types of Singing Bowls

About 50 different styles and types of bowls have been identified but there are only a few general styles that you will find in most stores. Most of the styles can be traced back to Tibet, India, Nepal, and Mongolia.

Thadobati

Thadobati is the oldest bowl form and some of the ancient bowls still around date back as far as the 15th century. They are characterized by high walls, flat bottoms, straight sides, and undecorated lips.

When played with a mallet, they can produce up to five octaves.

They are usually small to medium-sized and are popular acquisitions.

Their prices range between $60 and $560 as of 2021.

Jambati

Flat bottoms but curved sidewalls, an inward-facing lip, and hammer marks on the outside are distinguishing features of jambati bowls.

They can play up to four different octaves when a mallet is used.

Jambati is the heaviest and largest style and several craftsmen usually work together to produce one jambati bowl.

There are many antique examples still around. Their size made them great grain storage containers, which preserved them.

They can be quite expensive, ranging from $640 to $8,800. You will also need to purchase a cushion or mat to place the bowl on while playing it, due to its weight.

Naga

These small to medium-sized pedestal bowls are considered quite rare. Antique examples are usually found in great condition, which has led specialist collectors to suspect the naga bowls had a ceremonial usage such as holding offerings.

Due to the pedestal, the sound of a naga bowl can, unfortunately, sometimes be distorted. If you can find one to buy, it would be wise to test it first.

The price can range between $160 and $640.

Mani

Mani bowls, also known as mudra bowls, have flat bottoms but their lips face inward. They are short and fairly thick and can be small to medium-sized.

Their range is three octaves and their tone is considerably higher than other bowls.

It is believed mani bowls also had significance in rituals and ceremonies.

They can cost from $270 to $675.

Ultabati

They are also big and heavy bowls like jambati and produce sounds in the two low octaves. They can also provide the 'om' sound.

The outer walls are dark to black and the lips curve outward.

Ultabati bowls are generally quite expensive and their prices range from $700 to $2,000.

Manipuri

Manipuri bowls can be small to medium-sized. They are shallow with splayed rims.

Most beginners find them easy to play and they can produce a wide range of primary tones.

At prices ranging between $75 and $425, a manipuri bowl can be an affordable start to your singing bowl collection.

Lingam

Lingam, or lingham, bowls are rare. They are shallow bowls like the manipuri but they have a protrusion in the center that gives them a unique sound. They are not so easy to play.

An authentic lingam bowl can set you back anything between $400 and $1,900. Collectors warn against fakes, however. It is not difficult to rework some types of cheaper bowls to look like a lingam.

Remuna

Remuna bowls have thin, straight walls and can have beautiful artwork on the outside.

They are generally medium-sized and easy to play.

The price range is from $235 to $635.

How to Use Your Singing Bowl For a Sound Bath Meditation

Enjoying a next-level meditation experience with a singing bowl need not be an expensive exercise; in fact, you don't even need to leave your home if you own a bowl.

Decide how long you want to spend on your sound bath before you start (it can be as short as five minutes and still be effective), set your alarm, and relax!

Find a quiet, comfortable spot where you can relax without disturbances. Silence your phone and turn off any nearby computers.

Take three deep, slow breaths: In through your nose and out through your mouth.

And in...and out.

And in...and out.

Set the intention for your sound bath meditation. Possible intentions could be relaxing fully, grounding yourself, releasing anxiety, releasing anger toward someone specific, cultivating patience, strengthening compassion, or managing chronic pain.

Put the bowl flat on your one open palm without your fingertips touching it while holding the mallet in the other hand.

Activate the bowl by tapping it lightly on the side with the mallet. Be firm but gentle, even with a metal bowl. There is no need for a hard whack. Keep all your movements restful.

Hold your intention in your mind while you listen to the first chime of the bowl ringing out.

Start circling the outside of the bowl with the mallet to create a sustained singing sound or keep chiming it softly—do whatever feels right for you at that moment.

Keep the mallet in contact with the bowl and don't worry if the singing doesn't start immediately. It takes a while for the vibration to build.

Keep breathing deeply and calmly...in through your nose...out through your mouth.

Hold your intention in your mind.

Let the ringing flow over you and through you, freeing your energy to move through your body and mind as it should.

Do a mental scan of your body and notice any sensations there might be. Just notice them and let them go.

If any thoughts or mental pictures come to you while you're listening to the sound, allow them and let them go again. Gently bring your attention back to the sound and your breathing.

Breathe deeply and calmly...in through your nose...out through your mouth.

Keep doing this until the end of your sound bath session.

Before you still the bowl, express your gratitude for the experience to any spiritual figure you believe in. You can also thank the bowl for its service if that feels right for you.

Notice any mental or physical shifts that might have occurred during this time.

Still the bowl by touching it gently with your fingers and slowly return to your normal activities.

New or Old?

Both have their advantages and you have to decide whether you want to buy singing bowls as an investment or to play them. Antique bowls can be expensive but their sound quality is often superior to that of modern, machine-made bowls.

Older bowls were generally made with thinner bottoms than the modern versions and that, together with the wear and tear that 100 years or more of use brings, will make their warm, rich singing stand out among new bowls that tend to have sharper sounds.

If you want to buy old bowls as an investment, make sure their age and quality are authenticated by a reputable dealer.

Making the Decision to Buy

Ultimately the only real deciding factor should be whether the sound of the singing bowl speaks to you. Does it touch your heart and soul and move you?

Before buying, you should play the bowl, or at least listen to a good quality sound clip of it being played.

A good quality bowl will produce a strong, sustained sound with several harmonics and overtones. If the sound appears to flutter away, the quality of the bowl is not good.

The time it takes to get the bowl singing is not an indication of quality.

You also have to consider the size and weight of the bowl you want to buy. Is it a good fit for you, physically? You might want to play it for long sessions and if you have to hold something that is too heavy, it will be detrimental to the healing and de-stressing effect. Holding any object heavier than three pounds for long periods of time will get too uncomfortable.

You also have to be clear on your purpose. Are you going to use the singing for yoga classes, healing, meditation, grounding, or chakra balancing? Some bowls will be better than others for specific setups and uses. Low tones work better for grounding and meditation, for instance, but meditating in a small room will make it uncomfortable to work with a large bowl.

Similarly, take into account if you have to move meditation or yoga locations frequently. Lugging huge bowls around might just make you decide to give up on the exercise altogether.

If you plan to use the bowl/s for healing and chakra balancing, remember that huge bowls cannot be used near the head and ears. They have to be placed at the feet and you need smaller, lighter bowls to hold near the head and upper body. A crystal bowl with a handle is easier to move over the whole body.

A Buyer's Guide to Singing Bowls

The Reiki master and regular reviewer of healing equipment, Deborah from *The Light of Happiness*, provided her choice of the top nine brands to consider (The Light of Happiness, 2021a).

- Brand Janear International: Best Chakra Healing Singing Bowl. It is a handcrafted product from Nepal that provides great value for the price. Beginners can do well with this bowl as a starting point. The diameter is four inches and it resonates to the G-note, which is associated with the throat chakra. It comes with a nice-looking handmade cushion and a wooden mallet, as well as a handy carrying pouch.
- Brand Topfund: Best Quartz Singing Bowl. This is a green-colored frosted bowl that resonates with the F-note which is associated with the heart chakra. The bowl includes a rubber mat to stand on, a suede-covered rubber mallet that was designed specifically to be used with this bowl, as well as a heavy-duty carry case.
- Brand Nepamart: Best Singing Bowl Set. This is a beautifully decorated set of seven chakra bowls. Their diameters range from 2.8 to 5 inches. Each bowl has its own cushion and wooden mallet, and the chakra symbols are painted at the bottom. They are made of an alloy containing the traditional metals of copper and zinc.
- Brand Dharma Store: Singing bowls. These handmade bowls from Nepal are available in a variety of colors and are 4 inches in diameter. Each bowl contains zinc, nickel, copper, silver, mercury, brass, and gold. They resonate to an F sharp note.
- Brand Silent Minds: Best Singing Bowl With Cushion. The

bowl is made of bronze and can be bought in six different choices of appearance and color. The diameter is about 4 inches. The striker has wood on the one end and felt on the other, and an hourglass-shaped grip in the middle. The gold version is confirmed as associated with the crown chakra.

- Brand Dharma Store: Dharma Objects Bowl. This bowl includes a cushion and a two-sided mallet. The diameter of the bowl is slightly larger than 5 inches and it is quite sturdy. Eight lucky symbols are hand-crafted on the sides.
- Brand Resonance Imports: Best Singing Bowl with Mallet. If you want to go for a simple look, this could be a good choice. The handmade bowl comes in either a gold or a black version and it is unembellished. The choice of the cushion is either blue or black. The diameter is only 2.5 to 3 inches. It is not tuned to a specific frequency.
- Brand ShalinIndia: Singing Bowl. Another hand-painted bowl that can be purchased in gold, bronze, and silver finish. The diameter is 5 inches.
- Brand Maya Bodhi: Singing Bowl. The brass bowl is hand-hammered with an embossed image of a buddha in the bottom. It comes with a red silk cushion and a mallet. It is slightly heavier than other bowls with a 4-inch diameter, which gives it a rich, warm tone.

A bowl to avoid according to the review by *The Light of Happiness* is Hinky Imports' offering. The bowl cracked easily and the tone could not be sustained when the mallet was rubbed around the outside walls.

HOW TO START SOUND HEALING ON A BUDGET

Not everyone has unlimited resources available to start a sound healing practice, even if it is only on a small scale for personal use to start with. Some of the instruments and tools can be quite expensive and if you try to purchase everything, it might break the bank.

In this section, we'll look at the most effective way to get started while keeping your financial manager happy too.

There are a couple of instruments that come to mind immediately when thinking about sound healing and sound baths, but the cheapest one of them all is your own voice.

Humming, chanting, and singing can be the first instrument in your healing practice, without costing you anything. Some practice might be in order before you try this on anyone else; some people are naturally shy and find it difficult to perform in front of others. You won't know if it will work for you if you don't try it, though.

Rattles and shakers have been part of healing ceremonies since ancient times. They don't need to be expensive and you can even devise your own by using some dried plant material or seeds.

An animal skin drum adds a relaxing dimension to any healing session. Think about shamanic drumming, leading people gently into a highly receptive, trance-like state with the rhythmic pulses.

It is possible to find good quality animal skin drums for about $100 if you shop around.

Flutes have also been part of sound healing as far as human memory can go back. Depending on the flute maker you use, $140 can buy you a decent wooden flute that will last a long time.

Tuning forks have been discussed at length and you don't have to start with the expensive options.

Singing bowls have also been discussed, with a look at affordable options.

Chimes can be purchased for about $40 each. They bring an almost angelic quality to the sound bath.

If your budget allows it, you can acquire one instrument that will be a showstopper in your sound bath. A handpan, gong, and big crystal bowl all fall into this category.

You don't need all of these at once to get started. You can use what you have and can afford to get your sound healing journey going.

THE POWER OF HARMONIC HEALING

We are sound—pure, vibrating sound. We are even more than that, though. We are not only individual tones but also harmonic combinations of sound. Some harmonic resonant relationships sustain us, while others relax and balance us.

Harmonic healing explores the power of harmonics and their effects on us.

What Is a Harmonic Resonance?

Scientifically spoken, any sound consists of a fundamental tone and overtones. An overtone is any frequency greater than the fundamental tone.

If the value of an overtone is an integer multiple of the fundamental tone, the overtone is called a harmonic. The other overtones are fractional multiples of the fundamental tone.

Harmonics are always stationary waves but the other overtones are not.

The frequencies at which certain harmonic combinations vibrate have the power to heal the human body and mind.

We'll explore harmonic combinations and how to use them in more detail later in this section.

The History of Harmonic Healing

Ancient civilizations understood this basic concept about the power of sound and many of the old buildings still preserved reflect this.

Have you ever walked into a historic cathedral and felt the lofty silence lifting your soul without a sound? That is the power of a space built to harmonic proportions at work.

Many cultures and religions talk about the universe being created through a sound or spoken word. The ancient mystery schools of Greece, Rome, Egypt, India, and Tibet all based their teachings on the belief that vibration is the primary cause of the existence of the universe.

The priests were musicians too; the scientists were equally well versed in esoteric knowledge and music as in scientific principles. They had temples dedicated solely to the purpose of healing.

Fundamental to this belief were the teachings of Hermes Trismegistus. The spiritual and philosophical movement called Hermeticism dates back as far as the 1st century CE.

Hermes was believed to be a combination between the Greek god Hermes and the Egyptian god Thoth. His writings can be found in what is known as *The Hermetica*, a huge body of works spanning from about 300 BCE to 1,200 CE.

Hermes laid down seven main principles of the universe:

- The principle of Mentalism, according to which all is mind.
- The principle of Correspondence, according to which everything in heaven and on earth corresponds to each other.
- The principle of Vibration, according to which all is vibration.
- The principle of Polarity, according to which everything has a dual nature.
- The principle of Rhythm, according to which everything is in a constant state of flow.
- The principle of Cause and Effect, according to which everything happens to a law.
- The principle of Gender, according to which everything has both male and female sides and energies.

Both the principles of vibration and rhythm involve sound. According to Jonathan Goldman in his book *Healing Sounds: The Power of Harmonics* (1996), the principle of correspondence is also relevant to sound healing, although it doesn't appear so from the start.

Goldman explains this in terms of the rotation of planets that can be amplified mathematically to frequencies that the human ear could hear.

The healing temples utilized mathematically calculated intervals between notes. The calculations were pioneered by the Greek mathematician Pythagoras, who is known today as the father of modern geometry.

Using a monochord, he discovered the whole-number ratios between the notes.

Pythagoras believed the whole universe was one big monochord, with a string stretched between heaven and earth. The upper end was anchored in, what he called, absolute spirit. The lower end went down to, in Pythagoras' terminology, absolute matter.

Therefore, he postulated that everything in the universe can be explained in terms of harmonic ratios. He demonstrated harmonic relationships in nature, the planets, and the heavenly constellations.

Pythagoras was rumored to have been able to hear the vibrations of the planets. In modern astronomy, scientists have equated sounds to different planets and they appear to be in harmonic relationships to each other. Maybe Pythagoras could hear what no other human being has since heard without aid!

His teachings were passed on to his students at his monastery-like school in Crotona, in what is now the Italian region of Calabria. The school later burned down and many of his teachings were lost. Scientists have been searching through the years to understand his principles, based on what was preserved.

Notable among these scientists is the Swiss researcher Dr. Hans Jenny. He devoted his life to studying the effects of different frequencies on inorganic matter and called his work cymatics.

He clearly demonstrated that specific harmonies could rearrange inorganic matter into recognizable forms.

Harmonics in the Occult

The word 'occult' means that which is hidden. Studies of the occult are occupied with acquiring knowledge about the unseen things around us in the universe. It also relates to anything that is too subtle to be seen at first glance.

Harmonics also fall into this category in an auditory sense, because all the tones in a sound are not immediately apparent and they have to be studied for us to hear them.

The term occult is also used in conjunction with esoteric rituals and magical practices. The chanting that forms an integral part of many of these practices is all rooted in the belief that sound is powerful.

Specifically, hearing the overtones in a note is considered essential to raise a person to full consciousness and tune the whole being into a state of health and balance.

Harmonics in Shamanism

Shamanism is thought to be the oldest form of healing known to man and sound has always been an integral part of a shaman's work. For a discussion on the musical instruments favored by shamans, see the section earlier in the book about shamanic healing and journeying through the use of instruments.

Shamans communicate with the spirit world to do their work and to obtain knowledge. The voice is the most commonly used medium to achieve this.

Overtone chanting, or hoomi/xoomij/choomig, is a form of throat singing from the Tuvic region in Mongolia. It involves the singing of one note with two different and distinct pitches that are audible at the same time.

A bass-like, nasally droning sound forms the fundamental tone, while the overtone is a piercingly high sound that forms a melody above the droning.

The effect of this ghostly-sounding melody strengthened the ancient people's belief that shamans were in direct contact with supernatural powers.

Hoomi singing has since spread to many other cultures. The didgeridoo used by Australian aborigines produces the same type of sound.

Tibetan monks use it too in a form known as tantric harmonics. Chanting in their "one voice chords," they manage to produce three different notes at the same time.

Their chanting style started with a dream experienced by the Tibetan lama of 1433, in which he received this tantric voice. He was told in his dream that the voice is meant to unite the male and female sides of the divine energy to bring about a universal consciousness. It had to be used to show life in its fullness, with all the overtones that are normally only felt and not seen.

He taught the other monks to do it and they started a tantric monastery in Gyume. In the same century, at another monastery in Lhasa, the Gyuto Tantric College was founded.

Until China's 1950 invasion of Tibet, knowledge of this technique and the rituals of the monks were unknown to the outside world. Some monks escaped the invasion by fleeing to India, where they continued their practices.

Goldman talks about the effects of hearing these monks chant as "one of the most powerful sonic experiences imaginable" (1996). Musicologists have measured one instance of them singing and found the bass note to be two octaves below middle C. The frequency is 75.5 Hz. The deepest note reachable for any known professional opera singer is 150 Hz.

Harmonics in Meditation

Once you've attuned your ears and senses to the subtleties of overtones, a new listening experience opens up for you. It is suddenly possible to really hear the sounds around you again, in fine detail.

The whole consciousness seems to expand into a deeper and different awareness of the world, which includes actively and intuitively listening to other people.

The new way of listening also includes listening to your own inner voice with new attention. Meditation gets new meaning as you open up to receive the messages from your higher self and the creating spirit that pervades all things.

If you regularly listen to sounds that charge your brain positively, you will start to hear more of them. You will start hearing overtones in everyday sounds, opening up the path to a new level of awareness. Your imagination will get a new life, too, building a richness into your experience you never thought possible.

Most of the cranial nerves, including the vital vagus nerve, are linked to the ear. The vagus nerve affects the heart, the bronchii of the lungs, the gastrointestinal tract, and the larynx. Listening to harmonics will therefore influence our voices, breathing, heart rate, and digestion positively.

Creating the overtones yourself, actively involving you in the process, will trigger the relaxation response just like toning elongated vowels in mantras does. The relaxation response was described by Dr. Herbert Benson as a marked decrease in respiration, oxygen consumption, heart rate, and metabolism. Alpha waves in the brain increased.

One of the first Sufi leaders in the western tradition, Pir Vilayat Khan, said overtones are like a Jacob's ladder that the conscious mind can climb to the metaphysical realm to understand the higher truths.

Opening up to other levels of consciousness is an excellent way to do deep meditation. It can make it possible to become one with a sound, which is a key component of meditation. Sound becomes something that is alive with an energy of its own. Once you stop trying to control the sound but just allow it to be, you can travel on it to other planes of consciousness and find the source of the sound.

We can find answers that may have been eluding us and experience true oneness with others and the universe.

Harmonics in Healing

One can't help but ask the question of whether the future of healing lies in sound and specifically in harmonics. The American clairvoyant Edgar Cayce (1877-1945) predicted that sound would become the mainstream medicine of the future. That future might be closer than we think.

True healing is becoming whole in body and mind. Our minds and bodies are inextricably linked to each other. A healthy body with a fragmented mind will never lead to optimum fulfillment and vice versa. It is important to realize that the concept of a whole body does not refer to physical impairments; a paraplegic person can be as healthy as possible in the circumstances and still have a whole body, from an energetic perspective.

The intention of the healer, as discussed earlier in the book, is even more important when using the voice than when using an instrument or electronic device that is outside the body.

The Cymascope

At the forefront of scientific developments in harmonic healing is an electronic instrument that uses harmonic relationships to treat cancer patients. It is called a cymascope and has evolved thanks to the work of Dr. Jenny in cymatics (see the discussion about his work earlier on).

Physics and acoustics researcher John Stuart Reid developed the instrument to assist surgeons during cancer surgery. It can be difficult for the surgeons to distinguish between cancerous and non-cancerous cells and the cymascope clears up the confusion by creating cymatic images of cells.

The cymascope also rests on a 2002 discovery by Dr. James Gimzewski that all cells have their own sound (Price, 2021). The sound emitted by a healthy cell differs from that emitted by a cancer cell.

The cymascope makes the cells' 'songs' visible. Reid found that cancer cells have chaotic sounds, without any pattern to them. In contrast, healthy cells had harmonious sounds. When injected into the cymascope, two radically different pictures emerge. The cancer cells have none of the beautiful, symmetric patterns that form the healthy cells. Instead, they have skewed lines and a chaotic jumble of patterns.

The cymascope works through a light that is shone on the surface of water that is added inside the machine. The images are captured digitally. In a surgical environment, the camera feed will be sent directly to the surgeon's eyewear.

Reid envisages a device on the surgical spectacles that will be linked to a laser scanner, which the surgeon will move over the patient's body. The visual feed will go directly to the cymascope and when the surgeon looks down at the patient, the images created of the "cell songs" will be superimposed on the body. That will make it easier for the surgeon to decide where to cut.

Chakra Balancing

Author Dr. Randall McClellan developed a system to balance the chakras using the human voice. The series of fundamental notes range over two full octaves and are harmonically related.

McClellan associated the root chakra with a C-note, the sacral with a G, the solar plexus with the next C, the heart with the E, the throat with the G, the third eye with a B-flat, and the crown with the final C.

Mobilizing Cerebral Spinal Fluid

The free movement and flow of cerebral spinal/cerebrospinal fluid are important for overall health. It is a clear liquid that cushions the brain and spine, delivers nutrients, and removes waste.

The interaction between the fluid and the brain has to go on unhindered, otherwise, it could result in illness, brain damage, and ultimately death. Some people compare the cerebral fluid to the eastern concept of kundalini energy.

Goldman recounts a demonstration of the effects of harmonics on skull bones and cerebrospinal fluid during a meeting of his Sound Healers Association in Boston, in 1986. During his presentation, a guest speaker, chiropractor Dr. Harlan Sparer, checked the cranium bones of a person whom Goldman was toning harmonics to.

The bones of the skull not only moved during the toning, but the fluid moved easier while the respiratory rate slowed (1996).

Different Styles of Harmonic Overtone Singing

Besides the Mongolian throat singing and western overtone singing, there are several other parts of the world where the same technique is practiced. Not all of the singers create melodies; some only use intonation and resonance to achieve the results they aim for.

It is important to distinguish between overtone singing and real throat singing, although throat singing has become interchangeable with overtone singing since the 1990s. Genuine throat singing is done by narrowing the larynx and there are no overtones involved.

Umngqokolo: Xhosa Overtone Singing

The music found among the Xhosa tribe in the eastern part of South Africa is one example where both types of singing referred to above, can be found.

Male diviners do throat singing, which is a coarse, rough sound made in the throat, used as a kind of percussion. The women only practice a type of overtone singing that is also known as umngqokolo.

They make the sounds to imitate their bow musical instruments such as the 'umrhube' and 'uhadi,' believing it will help them to make contact with their ancestors to receive healing and spiritual guidance.

Songs of the Dani of Papua-New Guinea

The Dani, also spelled Ndani, live in the western part of New Guinea. They use overtone singing to contact the ancestors and obtain spiritual knowledge.

Cuncordu a Tenore From Sardinia

The 'tenore' singing is a specific style of folk music from the Barbagia region of the island of Sardinia. Cuncordu is Sardinian sacred music, used since ancient times to heal and teach.

It is performed by four men standing close together in a circle. The leader, or 'voche,' sings the solo melody in a regular voice. The second voice is called the 'mesuvoche' and he also uses his regular voice. The third and fourth voices, called the 'contra' and 'bassu' respectively, utilize overtone singing.

The Ratios of Harmonic Intervals

There are basic ratios that make up the main intervals.

1:1	Fundamental	55 Hz	A
2:1	Octave	110 Hz	A
3:2	Fifth	165 Hz	E
4:3	Fourth	220 Hz	A
5:4	Major third	275 Hz	C#
6:5	Minor third	330 Hz	E
7:6	Minor third	385 Hz	G
8:7	Major second	440 Hz	A

LEARNING TO DO OVERTONE SINGING YOURSELF

Our voices are the cheapest and most accessible instruments we have if we want to work and heal with sound. While not everyone can chant like a Tibetan monk, overtone singing is accessible to anyone who can speak.

Overtone singer Jill Purce said that the concentration demanded by, and the mechanism of doing overtone singing are, in her experience, the best way to utilize parts of the brain that never get used. That makes it possible to enter into the presence of pure spirit (Goldman, 1996).

A quick recap of a couple of the important concepts might be helpful.

Frequency

The number of cycles per second in the vibrational movement of a sound; the tempo at which the sound wave oscillates.

The Role of Frequency in Tuning

Musical instruments are tuned to specific frequencies. The standard tone, known as concert pitch, varies in different parts of the world and for different instruments and has changed through the years.

The most commonly used modern standard that came into use in 1939, is 440 Hz, corresponding to the A-note above middle C. The pitch was affirmed by the International Organization for Standardization in 1975 as the ISO 16 standard.

Since the beginning of the 21st century, many people have started advocating the use of 432 Hz instead of 440 Hz. No official changes have been made to the standard pitch yet.

Fundamental Tone

When you play a C-note on a piano, the first sound you hear is the C.

Overtones

The other sounds that are also present, besides the C. They are usually not audible to the average human ear.

Intervals

Overtones are mathematically related to each other and the difference between them is called an interval.

TONING THE VOWELS

The sounds of the vowels, 'aa,' 'ee,' 'ii,' 'oo,' and 'uu,' and the musical crossings from one to another when toning them, contain harmonics within them. Sounding 'aaa' has got a different quality to sounding 'eee' as in 'me,' for instance. The way every vowel is formed brings specific harmonics to the forefront in every respective sound.

Try to sing 'uuh,' 'ooo,' 'ohh,' 'aaa,' 'eye,' 'aye,' and 'eee' in one breath, at a pitch that is comfortable for you, and listen to the harmonics already contained within your voice without you even really trying.

Your pronunciation of each vowel and your mouth position when singing the crossings between the vowels will determine the exact intervals of the overtones produced. Generally, according to Goldman, the 'ooo'-sound helps to create the overtones of the octave and the fifth for the fundamental tone. The 'ohh'-sound will create overtones of the major third and the fifth intervals of the next octave. The 'ahh' or 'aye'-sound will help with the overtones of the seventh. Moving from 'ooo' to 'eee' will produce higher overtones with every new vowel (1996).

Contrary to what may feel right for you, you will be more successful with creating harmonic overtones if you pronounce less rigorously. Keep the sound in your throat and do not try to speak the vowels. Shape your mouth as if you are going to speak the vowel but do not actually enunciate it. The sound should be formed by changing the positions of your jaw, tongue, and cheeks.

Cupping one ear with your hand, in the beginning, will allow you to hear the sounds more clearly. If you hold the other hand with the palm facing you about two to three inches from your mouth, it will reflect the sound to your cupped ear, making it even easier to hear the different tones emerging.

Don't try to sing the initial, fundamental tone loudly. Keep it to the level of your regular speaking voice. The volume of the overtones is in an inverse proportion to the fundamental tone in the beginning. Focus the energy of the sound in your throat rather than outside your mouth and use all your vocal resonating cavities to amplify the harmonics. Harmonics are not about giving a performance in the regular sense; it is more about facilitating the production of the right sound that will allow the overtones to come into their own.

Sit comfortably before you start. With experience, it will become possible to sing harmonics while standing or even lying down, but in the beginning, you need the physical support to your diaphragm and breathing that sitting provides. Standing can also add an unnecessary layer of concentration to keep the right posture.

You might struggle a bit to distinguish the overtones in the beginning. The western ear is not generally trained to focus on individual tones, except if you are a musician or sound engineer. With practice, it will become second nature to you, however.

Begin by humming a 'mmm' sound on a pitch that comes naturally and comfortably for you. Keep the volume low. Concentrate the sound energy on your lips to create a strong vibrating sensation. You can test this by touching one finger to your lips—you should be able to feel them vibrating.

Move from 'mmm' to 'uuu' (as in 'moo') without breaking off the sound. Just move your lips. Then move on to 'ooo' (as in 'go'), to 'aaa', to 'iii' (as in 'my'), to 'aye' (as in 'may'), to 'eee'.

Open your lips just wide enough to allow the vowel to be audible after the 'mmm' and keep the vibration up.

Next, round your lips as if you want to start whistling. Imagine making a face like a fish when you open your lips.

Change your sound to 'mmmooorrrreee' (as in 'more') in one breath and draw it out as long as you can.

Take a nice deep breath and turn your attention to your nasal cavity next. It is important to project sound into the nasal cavity to produce overtones. It is not something that comes naturally to westerners and you will have to practice it.

One way of learning nasal projection is to put two fingers on either side of your nose while making a 'neeee' (as in 'knee') sound. You should be able to feel a vibration in your fingers. It is completely normal to experience a draining of your sinuses while doing this—you might want to keep a tissue handy!

Another good sound to practice next is 'nnnuuurrrr' (as in 'her'). First, get your nasal cavity vibrating on the 'nnnn' sound. Then add the 'uuurrr' part to 'nnnn.' The sound of the 'nnnn' will still be vibrating in the nose while the rest of the sound is added in the back of the throat.

The 'rrrr' part of the sound is produced by the tongue that has moved forward to vibrate close to the roof of the mouth. That is a particularly important placement to remember, as it helps to control the higher harmonic tones. Take note of the fact that the tongue is not actually touching the roof of the mouth but vibrating on saliva. If there is contact between the tongue and the mouth, the sound will be muffled and the vibrating of the tongue will be impeded.

Move your tongue back and forth in a straight line and listen to the changes in the sound. Find the one spot where the high tone, sounding like a small whistle, is the loudest. Once you're on that spot, change the shape of your mouth and enjoy the different harmonics you will be producing.

Another useful sound to practice is the 'nnnguuunnng' sound. It works with the muscle at the back of the throat that is called the glottis, to teach it to produce harmonics.

Start with 'nnnn' in the nasal cavity and then say the word 'gung' (as in 'tongue'). Go back to 'nnnn' and say the word 'gong.' Nasalize another 'nnnn' and say the word 'gang.' Do another nasal 'nnnn' and say the word 'ging' (as in 'sing').

Do the whole sequence now in one breath. Go from 'nnnngung' to 'nnngong,' to 'nnnngang,' to 'nnnging.' You are essentially keeping the nasal 'nnnn' sound going while intoning the other words. Become aware of the different harmonics that are produced from the back of your throat.

The next step is to try a combination of 'mmmooorrr,' 'nnnuuurrr,' and 'nnngong.' Do the whole sequence in one breath and listen to the changes in harmonics flowing from you.

Reverse the sequence to start with 'nnnngong' and end with 'mmmooorrr' next. You can also mix them up further and start with 'nnnuuurrr.'

According to Goldman, these three phonemes are the most useful for producing overtones. There are other combinations you can move on to, such as 'wwwooowww,' 'hhhuuurrreee' (like 'nnnnuuurrr' but with an added 'eee'), and 'oooeee.' The last one works best on a high pitch or in your falsetto voice.

Moving from 'uhhh' to 'eee' covers the whole spectrum of overtones (1996).

Your natural vocal range seems to influence the production of harmonics. If you are still struggling to produce them after practicing a while, try to shift your starting pitch a bit higher or lower and see if it makes a change. Harmonics are as individual as the singing voice itself.

You will probably hit on a specific phoneme that becomes your favorite. Focus your attention on it and work to make it louder. When you have succeeded in one harmonic line, it will be easier to practice all the others to perfection.

Try to do your practicing in a quiet environment to make it easier to hear the overtones. Your brain and ears are not used to the sounds and you might take a while to pick them up from among other sounds.

The resonance formed in your head by the sound of your voice (in the fundamental tone) also has to be mentally tuned out by your brain before you will be able to discern the overtones easily.

It can be helpful to record yourself during practice. We do not always hear ourselves as someone else does because some sounds get muffled to our own ears while traveling through bone. We can also forget to listen when we are concentrating so hard on producing the sounds.

Listening to a recording of yourself can also be a tremendous boost to your confidence because it might be difficult at first to believe that you really succeeded in making the sounds.

The key component is practice. Don't get disheartened if you don't get it right in a few days. It is not a process that happens without thinking and working on it because most of us have not been taught since childhood to experiment with sound. It is as much a brain shift as a physical sound-producing shift that you have to make. Be kind and gentle with yourself and remind yourself constantly that you can do it. It cannot harm you; in fact, it can only benefit you.

You have to have a positive attitude to harmonics when practicing, even if you are unsure if you will be able to master the technique. Set aside a minimum of 15 minutes every day, at a time and place where you can be calm and focused on your practice. Switch off any distractions such as a computer and put your phone on airplane mode if you're keeping it on to record yourself.

Don't rush through the phonemes. Tone them deliberately and mindfully. Take some time between exercises to reflect on what you have achieved and any sensations you might feel anywhere in your body. Your heart rate, blood pressure, respiration, and skin temperature might change.

If the toning brings up any mental images or memories, take a moment to notice them too. Don't dwell on any emotions, just acknowledge them and let them go. You are healing.

Keeping a journal can be helpful in tracking your restorative journey. Once you put a sensation, thought, memory, or emotion into words on paper, it is out of your mental way and you can move on.

Many traditions view harmonics as sacred sounds. You now have the ability to create them in your own life and body. Accept them with joy and respect for the immensely wonderful way the universe works. Enjoy their rejuvenating and balancing power!

A SLIGHTLY MORE SIMPLIFIED APPROACH

A more condensed approach from a slightly different angle is also effective but it might take a while longer to fully master harmonics this way. Make sure your trachea and vocal cords are well hydrated because a dry mouth and throat will make it difficult to sing.

- Relax your lips and jaw. If you find that difficult, choose any note at a pitch that is comfortably mid-range for you and drone on it. Choose a vowel sound such as 'aa' or 'oo,' inhale, and drone the vowel sound on a full, slow exhale.
- Do this as many times as you need to feel fully relaxed. You should be able to hang your jaw without any sensation of tension or tightness in your neck and throat muscles.
- Open your mouth and hold your tongue just under the roof of your mouth. Make an 'rrr' or 'lll' sound without touching your tongue anywhere against your mouth. If it brushes against the roof of your mouth occasionally that is fine, just lower it slightly again, so as not to dampen the sound.
- Holding your tongue in this position, change your sound to 'oo.' Try to sing it in your chest voice, as deep as you can. It's like saying the word 'cool' to someone in a bass voice.
- Now move the body of your tongue backward and forward (or up and down, if that feels more intuitive to you), without changing the position of the tip of your tongue. Think of it as alternating between an 'r' and an 'l' sound without moving your whole tongue. It will take some time to get used to doing this—be patient and take it slow.
- Slowly change the position of your lips to an 'ee' sound while still keeping your tongue in the same spot.
- Move your lips again to form a 'uu' sound (as if saying "see you" without the 's').
- Do it slowly and listen to the changes in resonance in your mouth.
- You are now ready to put it all together: Place your tongue near to the roof of your mouth as if you are going to say an 'rrr'; move the position of your lips slowly between the 'ee' and 'uu' sounds.

- Now curl your tongue up, backward, and away from your lips.
- When you hear the overtones emerging, stop moving your mouth and hold the position.

Make sure you sing from your chest and not your head. A head voice is higher in pitch and you don't feel the resonance as clearly in your body as with a chest voice.

When you have the basics going smoothly, you can create melodies by changing your fundamental tone and moving your lips.

Listening to recordings and watching videos of overtone singers can also help you. Practice your mouth positions in front of a mirror to make sure you imitate the videos correctly.

✣ 8 ✣

MANTRA MAGIC

Mantras are words or phrases that are repeated during meditation to aid concentration. They originated in the Indian tradition, where it was viewed as a sacred utterance.

Instructors in Hinduism and Buddhism gave personal mantras to their students when they were initiated.

The use of mantras has become much more generalized but it is still just as useful to focus the mind. They are not meant to silence all thoughts completely but rather to expand the mind, to increase awareness of outside stimuli and emotional sensations without getting involved.

THE ANATOMY OF A MANTRA

Although many people understand a mantra as an intention or an affirmation, it is much more than that. The word is made up of the two parts 'man' and 'tra.'

'Man' comes from the Sanskrit word 'manas' that refers to the linear thinking mind, while 'tra' means 'crossing over.' A mantra is a way to help the mind cross over into a state of deep relaxation, meditation, and awareness.

Mantras can be anything that doesn't consist of distracting content but they often don't mean anything. The ones without meaning are merely aids to reach a heightened level of awareness about the self and our responses to our sensations and surroundings (Thorp, 2021).

Other mantras refer to deities and petition them for certain things (Atkins, 2015).

The History

The earliest mantras date from at least 3,500 years ago. They were composed in Vedic Sanskrit, which was an Indo-European language that existed in India long before the advent of writing.

The Veda refers to a collection of hymns and verses that were regarded as sacred. People believed the words were given to the seers by the gods themselves (Feuerstein, 2011).

In early Hinduism, mantras were used to solemnize rituals. Each mantra was associated with a specific ritual. The purposes of the rituals were to solve concrete, everyday problems such as finding missing cattle.

Over time, the concepts of abstract virtues and intentions developed.

The first mantra was om/ohm/aum—there are several different spellings of the mantra. The mantra refers to the origins of every-thing and the creator and is prefixed to all Hindu prayers (Feuerstein, 2011).

The Science

A study done by scientists in Israel confirmed what yogis have been saying for years: Repeating a word or phrase slows down a part of the brain that deals with, among other things, our response to stressors.

Activity in the brain quiets down, eliminating any processes that compete with the repetition of the mantra. What the researchers call "high-level cortical responses" are reduced, producing a pervading calming effect (Berkovich–Ohana et al., 2015).

For healing, this means that external stimuli that compete with the mind's focus on the healing activity are muted, so to speak. Physical processes also calm down enough that they don't interfere with the mind's healing work.

The sound of the mantra, whether spoken audibly or silently, creates vibrations that aid in healing.

The healing effect of meditation was proven in a study in which eight people older than 60 with memory loss were asked to do a Kirtan Kriya meditation for 12 minutes every day, keeping it up for eight weeks. After the eight weeks, key points in their brains and cognitive performance were assessed and compared to the beginning of the study.

Significant improvements in memory and mood, among other things, were found (Moss et al., 2012).

Types of Mantras

There are three main types of mantras.

- A bija (pronounced 'beej') is a Vedic seed mantra. Bija mantras are seen as the core sounds that are associated with deities. It is believed they are endowed with spiritual powers to grant wishes. They are often incorporated into other mantras to boost their effectiveness. Bija mantras are used to open and balance the chakras (Yogapedia, 2017).
- Saguna mantras are believed to have the power to give rise to the form of deities. The Sanskrit word 'saguna' means having qualities associated. Saguna mantras are used to invoke specific deities to obtain something from them, such as their protection (Yogapedia, 2017).
- Nirguna mantras are abstract philosophical statements. The Sanskrit word 'nirguna' means being without form. The mantra that is seen as the original creation sound, 'aum,' is a nirguna. Nirguna mantras are the oldest and originate from Vedic texts (Yogapedia, 2017).

SOME WELL-KNOWN MANTRAS

If you've ever wondered what words like 'om' and 'padme' mean and what they are used for, this section is for you.

Om Mani Padme Hum

This is one of the best-known mantras in the world. Its origins are in India and Tibet.

Many Tibetan monks chant the words thousands of times every day, as part of their rituals. The Dalai Lama translated the words as "the jewel is in the lotus" (Atkins, 2015).

In the yogic tradition, the lotus symbolizes the power of transformation out of the mud into a magnificent flower. Chanting the mantra means affirming the power to do what is necessary to transform one's life out of darkness and ignorance into wisdom, grace, and beauty.

Part of the appeal of this mantra lies in the universal aspect. At any given time, many people all over the world are chanting the words at the same time. That creates a link to all who have strived in the past to move on from ignorance to wisdom, and to all those who, in the future, will keep on doing that.

Om Namah Shivaya

This is a salutation to the god Shiva, who is associated with transformation through destruction. It speaks of finding peace and solace despite knowing that destruction is unavoidable.

It is often referred to as the five-syllable mantra, evoking the five elements of existence according to the Hindu and Vedic traditions: Fire, air, water, earth, and space.

So Hum

This is considered to be what is known as a breath mantra. The philosophical meaning of the words is considered to be "I am that" but the mantra can also be paired with inhalations and exhalations only, without contemplating any deeper meaning.

In the yogic tradition, it is believed that So Hum vibrates on the same frequency as Om, the sound of creation. It is said to bring expansion to the consciousness, symbolizing the constant state of change that we and creation are in.

When used as an aid to breathing, inhalation is done on 'hum' and exhalation on 'sa' (Atkins, 2015).

Aham Prema

Loosely translated from Sanskrit, the mantra means "I am divine love." When chanting the words, the person affirms that he/she is aligning him/herself with the purity of divine love (Yogapedia, 2017).

TRANSCENDENTAL MEDITATION

Transcendental meditation falls into the category of no-concentration meditation. It is a way of allowing the mind to move freely to the stillness which is already there, without focusing on anything specific.

Proponents of the technique believe it is, among other things, better at reducing anxiety and drug-dependent behaviors, and decreasing blood pressure (The Meditation Trust, n.d.).

It differs from mindfulness meditation in that there is no effort involved to focus the mind on the breath or something else.

By allowing the mind to roam while chanting a mantra, brain waves change to an alpha pattern. Alpha waves are associated with deep relaxation and restful alertness (The Meditation Trust, n.d.).

Origins

Transcendental meditation comes from the Vedic tradition. The Indian sages practiced meditation for years but the techniques and knowledge were not accessible to the general population.

In 1953, a famous guru named Brahmananda Saraswati, called Guru Dev by his followers, set his student by the name of Maharishi Mahesh Yogi the task to spread the knowledge of meditation all over the world.

In 1958, Maharishi Mahesh Yogi traveled to the USA and Europe with his message. He was so successful that meditation became a well-known and often-practiced activity in the West. The pop group The Beatles even went to India in 1968 to study with him.

By the time of his death in 2008, Maharishi Mahesh Yogi had

certified more than 40,000 meditation teachers and established numerous transcendental meditation centers all over the world (TMHome, n.d.).

What's In the Name?

Maharishi Mahesh Yogi coined the term 'transcendental' to distinguish the meditation technique he was teaching from other types of meditation.

He wanted to emphasize the process of transcending the ordinary thought patterns of the mind, to reach perfect stillness.

Transcendental Meditation Mantras

The mantras that are silently repeated during transcendental meditation are personalized, given to a student by an instructor. The instructor follows the guidelines laid down by Maharishi Mahesh Yogi.

During this type of meditation, the mantra and its sound are not used as a focal point but rather as a vehicle to transport the mind effortlessly into deeper realms.

To be a transcendental meditation mantra, it has to be a meaningless sound to bypass the cognitive mind. It also has to resonate with the sound of creation, 'om,' to attract the mind into seeking greater happiness and harmony (TMHome, n.d.).

The mantras are Sanskrit sounds that are believed to produce healing for the whole body and mind.

Students of the technique are required to keep their mantra secret, to preserve its power for them personally when used correctly.

The mantra is always used silently, to allow both the body and the mind to sink into a deep state of rest. Speaking the mantra aloud engages muscles and occupies the mind, which will prevent the person from reaching natural silence.

❧ 9 ❧

SOUND-POWERED GUIDED
MEDITATIONS

T he relationship between sound and meditation is a powerful one. Both of these healing giants do a sterling job on their own but together, their effects are amplified.

Many experts have created sounds and music specifically for meditation and a lot of it is available for free on websites such as Youtube. There are also numerous free apps for mobile devices.

Any sound can, however, be used for a sound meditation if you are in the right frame of mind.

In this chapter, we'll first explore why sound and meditation are such good partners, before moving on to some guided meditations you can try. The scripts of the meditations are fully written out, so you can easily read and record the lines for yourself on your cell phone. If you add your own music or downloaded sounds, you can sit or lie back and enjoy the benefits of the meditations whenever you feel like it.

SOUND AND MEDITATION: PERFECT PARTNERS

Just like meditation alters some aspects of brain function, sound does too. Does that sound far-fetched to you? We'll explore both statements in more depth before we get to the meditation scripts.

Sound

The world of sound, and its effect on us, is so profound that scientists discover new facets all the time. Talking about it is like turning a gemstone to catch the light in all possible ways, without repeating any of the information already discussed earlier in the book.

Whether you listen to sounds of nature, music, your own voice, or even sounds that are normally perceived as intrusive noise, your brain responds to the sounds and your intentions while listening (MacMillan, 2017).

Scientists from the Brighton and Sussex Medical School in England conducted functional magnetic resonance image (fMRI) scans on the brains of 17 young adults while they listened to nature sounds. The participants were between 17 and 34 years of age, with no prolonged medication use, or history of significant physical or mental illness.

Their brains were monitored through four separate sets of soundscapes of just more than five minutes each. While listening, they had to perform a monitoring task on a computer screen that required a low level of attention.

Besides the scans, the participants also reported on their subjective experiences of the soundscapes and the monitoring task.

The scientists found a remarkable difference between the attention spans and heart rates of those who listened to nature sounds, as compared to the participants who did not have nature sounds to listen to.

Regarding brain activity, the fMRI scans showed a shift in the region of the brain where the activity to perform the monitoring task took place after listening to nature sounds, as compared to those participants who did not listen to the soundscapes before completing the same monitoring task. The main brain activity moved from the anterior, or front, part to the posterior, or back, part (Gould van Praag et al., 2017).

Put simplistically, this implies that cognitive actions moved from being purely rational to becoming more visually guided. Expressed differently, the focus of those people who listened to sounds of nature was turned outward, while the focus of the other group was turned inward—a brain pattern that is associated with stress.

That implies further that listening to sound can alter the way we see and interpret the world.

Meditation

Although meditation has been known for centuries and many people swear by its effectiveness, the medical community has now found scientific proof of the changes brought about by the practice.

Through the use of fMRI scans, brain activity could be mapped and studied, providing visuals of how we respond to meditation.

A study done in Italy found that meditation leads to neurobiological modifications in people's self-awareness, attention, memory, as well as the regulation of their emotions and responses to stimuli. After as little as 20 minutes of meditation, alpha waves that indicate rational reasoning decreased, and theta waves that show deep relaxation, increased. This pattern persisted for a significant time after the meditation session was done. According to the scientists, the effect is similar to what people who exercise regularly experience (Boccia et al., 2015).

There is no right or wrong way to meditate. It is something you can do in the way that suits you best. Guided meditations, scripts, and other information materials are simply opening the way for your own experiments.

In guided meditation, someone talks you through the process. All you have to do is close your eyes and follow the voice.

Unguided meditation happens in silence and the only guide is your thoughts.

Meditation can be focused on relaxation and calming, solving a specific issue, or gaining insight into a situation or problem. Your meditation can also incorporate all these elements in one session.

There are various styles of meditation, incorporating different types of sounds, or silence.

If you choose sound, you can use soundscapes of nature, a voice, mantras, music such as solfeggio frequencies and binaural beats, or ambient sounds. You can even use everyday noises—one of the scripts later in this chapter deals with noise.

Humming is another powerful type of meditation.

To help focus the mind, meditations usually start with a mental body scan. It is like doing an awareness inventory of your body, from head to toe. That brings all sensations, tensions, or aches to your attention. You can then relax and send healing energy to every part of the body that needs it.

The next part of the meditation deals with the main focus of the session, whether it is an intention or a problem that needs to be solved.

Let's put your newfound knowledge into practice now!

SCRIPTS FOR GUIDED MEDITATIONS

Below are some scripts for meditations, designed to help you cultivate mindfulness and address common problems for healing.

It will work best if you record the scripts and play them back to yourself. A couple of tips for successful meditation script recording are:

- Don't read too fast. What feels like slow reading sounds different when you listen to it. Allow at least two to three breaths between every line.
- Many people don't like listening to their own voices. Don't let that put you off, though. Subconsciously, we often listen better to suggestions given by ourselves than by others. That way the suggestions don't feel like orders.
- Read in a calm voice, pausing in the middle of phrases whenever it feels comfortable to do so.
- Say the words clearly without over pronouncing anything.
- Play the audio back at a low enough volume to be calming, but loud enough that you can listen to it without straining.

Turning Noise Into Healing Sounds

Would you believe that everyday noises that are usually perceived as annoying can be used in meditation to bring about healing and balance?

It is not the sound itself that is bad; it is our perception of the sound that gives it a 'bad' quality. If we change our attitude toward the sound from aversion to curiosity, the sound is just as effective in meditation as a soothing nature soundscape.

Find a comfortable place to sit or lie down.

Don't cross your ankles and stretch your legs out straight if you're lying down. If you're sitting, keep your feet flat on the floor next to each other.

Relax your arms and hands, either in your lap or next to you on the bed.

Close your eyes if you feel comfortable doing so, or direct a soft gaze toward the horizon or some point ahead.

Breathe in deeply on the count of four...hold it for two...and exhale on the count of four.

Become aware of all the sounds you can hear. The sounds are outside but also inside your body.

Hear your breathing.

Hear your heartbeat.

Hear your blood rushing.

Hear any sounds your stomach might be making.

And breathe in.

1...2...3...4.

Hold your breath.

1...2.

Let it out through your mouth.

1...2...3...4.

And again...breathe in.

1...2...3...4.

Hold your breath.

1...2.

Let it out through your mouth.

1...2...3...4.

Now become aware of sounds outside. Do you hear car horns blaring? Do you hear people talking? Do you hear traffic roaring? Do you perhaps hear a lawnmower or a leaf blower somewhere? Do you hear children playing or a baby crying? Is there a plane flying over?

Turn your attention to your house. Is there a television playing? Are there cell phones ringing? Is someone cleaning the house or doing something in the kitchen? Is there a microwave beeping? Are there dogs barking or parrots whistling?

Notice all these sounds without emotion. Don't resent them and don't try to block them. Open your mind to them and follow them. Be curious about them. Let them be. Listen.

[Pause]

Feel your whole being becoming light and allow your awareness to be carried on the waves of the sounds. Feel all the tension stored in your body drop away and stay behind while you drift on the currents of sound.

Don't think about anything, just drift and observe and relax.

And breathe in...hold for a moment...and breathe out.

Feel the warmth and incredible lightness of being at peace with yourself and your surroundings.

Gradually return your attention from the outside to the inside of your mind and body again.

Allow the sound waves to float into your body and remove all discomfort and tension. Feel the restful peace gently push all doubts and worries out of your mind until you're completely quiet inside.

Stay in this stillness for as long as you like.

[Pause]

Turn your awareness slowly back to the outside world when you are ready.

Move your limbs and open your eyes.

Relieving Physical Pain

People who experience deep relaxation as in a state of meditation stand the best chance to manage chronic pain. Much of the success of a pain relief meditation depends on whether you accept or fight your pain.

Pain is the body's way of telling you there is an imbalance somewhere that needs to be addressed. You need to fully accept that as your body's loving way to guide you and work with it. Only then will you be able to transform the pain and find relief.

For this meditation, you can choose any nature sounds that you find soothing and relaxing. Sounds such as surf breaking, water flowing over stones, or soft rain falling can all work well, depending on your preference. Using earphones will make it easier to focus on the sounds and avoid distractions.

Sit or lie in a comfortable position in which you experience the least pain and discomfort.

Focus on the sounds of nature you hear and try to exclude other sounds for now.

Next, focus on your breathing. Without forcing anything, start breathing from your abdomen instead of your chest.

Now stand back mentally and observe your physical sensations. Where are you feeling pain? How intense is it? Does it bring a color, taste, form, or smell to your mind?

Locate your tension. Take note of where it is stored and how it makes that part of your body feel. Does the color, taste, form, or smell of the tension differ from the pain?

Continue breathing smoothly and deeply, exhaling fully.

Hold the picture of your pain and tension before you. Don't judge and don't try to change or fight anything. Simply observe. It is what it is in this moment.

As each moment passes, observe how subtle changes take place. No moment is exactly the same as the previous one.

Now, try to look at your pain and tension with acceptance. If you have a personal soothing color, try to change the colors of the discomforts to that shade.

If you feel yourself tensing up with the effort, ease up and breathe first. Then try again. This is not a race or a test.

Repeat some affirmations for pain management, in any order:

- *I accept myself*
- *I accept my pain*
- *I accept my tension*

Relax for a moment and just observe again. Breathe in deeply and exhale fully.

Turn your mind's eye back to your pain and tension. Did anything change? Did you manage to change anything, even if ever so slightly?

Now picture your pain again and imagine it is a cold patch, instead of a painful one. Breathe in deeply and breathe cool air out into the pain, borne on the waves or wind you are listening to.

Visualize the cooling sensation moving in under the pain and replacing discomfort with a pleasant tingle.

Experience the pleasant sensation growing, taking over the painful area and allowing you to relax your tired muscles that were clenched to fight the pain.

Take a deep breath in...and let it out.

And in...and out.

And in...and out.

Choose a focus word to repeat while you keep on breathing calmly, such as restful.

Breathe in and exhale on 'restful' in your mind. Allow yourself to drift away on your focus word peacefully. When other thoughts try to intrude, gently bring your focus back to 'restful.'

In...restful...out.

In...restful...out.

In...restful...out.

Keep this up for as long as you like. You don't have to make anything happen and you are under no pressure to produce anything. Just relax into your restfulness.

When you are ready to return to your regular activities, take a moment to become aware of the sensations in your body again. Take note of how relaxed your muscles are and how still everything inside you is.

Memorize this feeling and take it with you when you slowly open your eyes. Move your arms and legs slightly while you breathe in deeply once more. Do a gentle stretch on the exhale and experience a feeling of alertness returning to your body and mind.

Letting Go of Anxiety

Anxiety and panic can take many disguises in our lives and they also show up in physical symptoms such as digestive problems or migraines. It is a natural part of the body's fight or flight response.

Sometimes, however, anxiety occurs without a clear trigger and that can become problematic and even debilitating, in severe cases.

Fortunately, meditation and sound can help. The script below deals with general anxiety. A couple of adaptations you can use to target specific places in your body where anxiety manifests are added at the end. Simply substitute a targeted section for the general part, if you need to.

If you feel like combining this meditation with solfeggio frequencies, listen to the universal 528 Hz frequency for rewiring the neural pathways in the brain to release anxiety or 396 Hz that promotes the cleansing of fear and feelings of guilt. The former frequency is associated with the solar chakra and the latter with the root chakra.

Find a comfortable spot to sit or lie down. Keep your arms by your sides when lying down, or comfortably relaxed in your lap when sitting. Keep your legs and ankles uncrossed to help improve blood flow.

Close your eyes if you feel comfortable doing so. If it makes you feel more anxious, fix your unfocused gaze somewhere ahead.

You are safe and protected in this moment and you can relax.

Breathe in deeply, from your abdomen. Keep your shoulders down and relaxed, do not pull them up to breathe.

If the anxiety makes it difficult to pull air in deeply because you feel constricted, do not fight it. Just take a breath as deeply as you can in the moment and savor the sensation.

Breathe in again...and out.

And in...and out.

Fill your lungs as deeply as you can with air and allow it to expand the feeling of restriction inside your body and mind.

Breathe in...and out.

And in...and out.

Let go of the tightness and trembling. Allow the breath to push it out and away.

There is nowhere else you need to be right now...nowhere you have to rush to...no demands on your time. You are in a safe, restful place where you are welcome and loved.

You have nothing to feel guilty about because you are in the right place and

*time for you. You deserve this time to relax and to fill your mind and soul with
new energy to function at your best.*

You are doing the right thing. You are looking after your health.

Breathe in again...and out.

And in...and out.

*While you keep breathing calmly and deeply, become aware of the sensa-
tions in your body. Do not judge and do not evaluate. There is nothing wrong.
Things are as they are. Observe them.*

*Where do you feel physical sensations? Are there aches? Are there discom-
forts? Where are they? Don't try to change them, just note them.*

Breathe in again...and out.

And in...and out.

*Start at the top of your head. Do you have a headache? Does your head feel
tight, like there's a band around it?*

Does your neck hurt and feel tight?

*How about your face and jaw? Are you frowning? Are you clenching your
teeth? Do any teeth hurt?*

*Move down to your shoulders. Are they aching or tired? Are they
bunched up?*

*Do your chest and rib cage feel tight and constricted? Does it hurt to
breathe deeply?*

*Observe the middle of your body. Does it feel hollowed out and uncomfort-
able? Does it feel tight? Does it hurt in any way?*

*Is there any discomfort in your abdomen? Do you feel nauseous? Do you feel
hungry but you can't put a name to what you're looking for? Do you feel
bloated and heavy?*

Move your awareness to your hips. Is there any tension or pain?

Breathe in again...and out.

And in...and out.

*Observe your legs and feet. Are they relaxed? Are your toes turned up or
are they relaxed?*

*Now that you know where the tight spots are, go back to them, one by one.
Hold one place of tension in your mind while breathing in. As you breathe out,
send the breath into the tightness. Visualize the muscles gradually letting go of
the tension as the breath fills them and opens them up.*

Feel the pleasant warmth of relaxation spreading across your body.

Imagine you are breathing in pure calmness and relaxation, and breathing out tension, tightness, and heaviness.

Breathe in calmness...and tension out.

And calmness in...and tension out.

Keep replacing tightness and discomfort with open, relaxing calmness. Feel all the trembling inside you stop, leaving behind a blissful silence in which you float, feeling light and relaxed.

Breathe in calmness...and tension out.

And calmness in...and tension out.

* Now go back to the places in your body where you previously felt tightness. Do they feel different now?

Take as long as you need to do this.

[Pause]

If there are places that have not released their tension yet, keep sending calmness with your inhalations and letting tightness out with your exhalations.

Breathe in calmness...and tension out.

And calmness in...and tension out.

Savor the feeling of softness and warmth that is coming over your whole body. Snuggle into it. You deserve it.

Feel the hardness that was packed into your core melting, becoming soft and warm.

Rest in the soft warmth, enjoying it, savoring it.

[Pause]

Now become aware of your thoughts. Did they change when the sensations in your body changed? Are they calmer, slower, fewer?

Allow your mind to drift in any direction it wants. Don't focus on anything, just let your thoughts wander. See what they bring you, without responding in any way.

Breathe in quietness...and noise out.

And quietness in...and noise out.

Take as long as you want to enjoy this state of quiet relaxation. Keep breathing deeply and calmly.

[Pause]

* Anchor the memory of this feeling in your mind and the fibers of your

being. Whenever you feel anxiety coming on, remember the feeling and allow it to flood you again with calmness and comforting warmth.

Start returning to the awareness of your surroundings. Slowly allow the sounds and sensations of your physical world to penetrate your consciousness again.

Move your limbs slightly. Keep breathing deeply and calmly.

Open your eyes when you are ready.

Anxiety in the stomach

Replace the general script from * to * with the following:

Direct your loving, calm attention to your stomach. Become aware of how it feels. Does it feel knotted up and tight? Do you feel empty and hollow? Do you have any pain? Do you feel nauseous or otherwise uncomfortable? Do you feel hungry without wanting food and not knowing what it is you really are looking for?

Describe your stomach sensations in your mind. Give them words and pictures. Allow them to be and accept them. Think of them as messengers from yourself who came to show you where you need healing.

Now that you have your mind pictures, you can let them float away.

Return your attention to your breathing. Breathe in as deep as you can without forcing or pulling your shoulders up— try to do it to a count of four.

1...2...3...4...

Hold the breath for a count of two.

1...2...

Let it out through your mouth to the count of four.

1...2...3...4.

And breathe in.

1...2...3...4...

Hold the breath for a count of two.

1...2...

Let it out through your mouth to the count of four.

1...2...3...4.

Feel your breath moving on the sounds of the music around you and allow the sound to penetrate the tight ball in your stomach. Allow the sound to gently work its way through the turmoil and discomfort you feel, leaving calm silence in its wake.

Let the sound pick you up and float you on a cushion of relaxed peace. Feel the music move into every part of your body, leaving behind the same gentle, restful, light sensation.

And breathe in.

1...2...3...4...

Hold the breath for a count of two.

1...2...

Let it out through your mouth to the count of four.

1...2...3...4.

Return your attention to your stomach. Does it feel soft and open now? Does it feel calm and ready to accept life and its experiences again?

Anxiety showing in fidgeting hands

Replace the general script from * to * with the following:

Now return your attention to your hands. Were they still up to now, or did they move? If they want to fidget, allow them to do so now. Fidget all you want for 20 seconds.

[Pause]

Now stretch your hands and fingers as wide as is comfortable for you. Open them slowly and calmly...stretch them...stretch your arms out too. Hold the stretch for a moment or two...and release.

Now ball your hands into tight fists, as tight as you can squeeze them...hold...and release.

Open your hands again and stretch them, spreading your fingers wide and stretching your arms...hold them...and release and let your hands and arms go limp.

Feel the warm, relaxed sensation in your hands now that they had a good stretch. They might even tingle a bit.

Let your arms and hands lie loose at your sides or in your lap. Savor the stillness that has come into your hands. Become fully aware of the calm, relaxed sensation of heaviness in them.

Each time you want to move your hands, feel how they are too heavy to move. They are just...too...relaxed.

Your hands and your arms are getting heavier...and more relaxed...they are growing to hold more heaviness.

The heavy feeling is pleasant and reassuring. You are calm, restful, and happy.

Breathe in deeply...and exhale.

And breathe in...and exhale.

Now fill your mind with a picture of the color blue. It doesn't need a form, it's just blue. See the blue in the most relaxing shade you can imagine.

Visualize the relaxing blue moving into your hands and arms...representing the still, calm heaviness.

When you feel the need to fidget coming on, imagine the color blue and experience the sensation of serene stillness and relaxation.

Breathe in deeply...and exhale.

And breathe in...and exhale.

Immerse yourself totally in the color blue for a few moments...take as long as you want.

[Pause]

Just breathe. Don't think about anything, just feel your calm, deep breathing. When you want to fidget, imagine the color blue and instantly experience the stillness returning to your hands and arms.

Whenever you feel like fidgeting in the future, know you can picture the color blue and feel your hands relax.

Breathe in deeply...and exhale.

And breathe in...and exhale.

Anxiety showing in clenching the jaw

Many people complain of waking up with toothache or headache because they grind their teeth and clench their jaws while they sleep. Clenching can also become subconscious behavior while concentrating on a stressful task, increasing the stress already being experienced.

Replace the general script from * to * with the following:

Zoom in on your mouth and jaw now and become aware of all the sensations there.

Are you clenching your teeth now? Are your teeth, jaw, or gums hurting? Do you feel any tightness in the muscles around your jaw and the area of your throat? Does it feel difficult to swallow? Do you have any earaches?

Don't measure or judge, just observe.

Breathe in deeply now and when you exhale, send the breath into your jaw. And breathe in...and exhale.

Take the waves of the music you are listening to and the sound of your voice reading this script with your breath into your jaw and feel how they lift and replace the tension there.

Feel a coolness spreading in your mouth and the tight, achy feeling disappear.

Now empty your mind for a few moments and just...breathe.

Breathe in deeply...and exhale.

And breathe in...and exhale.

Next, tense your jaw and hold your teeth together lightly. Not enough to cause discomfort, just lightly, and hold for a few moments.

Notice the sensations in your face and jaw. Notice where muscles are tense now and if any aches returned.

Then let go slowly, savoring the loosening sensation.

Breathe in deeply...and exhale.

And breathe in...and exhale.

Tense your jaw again and hold your teeth together a bit firmer. Not painful, but tighter. Notice the changes in your muscles and become aware of the sensations that bring. Hold the clench for a few moments.

Let go of the tension all at once.

Breathe in deeply...and exhale.

And breathe in...and exhale.

Let your lower jaw drop and hang slightly. Feel the free, relaxed feeling.

Now, open your mouth widely, as widely as you can. Feel as if you're going to yawn and pull the muscles in your cheeks up too.

Relax everything, letting your mouth close and your muscles become loose once again.

Hold your jaw in a comfortable position and memorize the feeling.

Know that, from now on, when your jaw feels tight, this is the feeling you can come back to.

Take a deep breath, exhale, and lean into this loose, relaxed feeling for as long as you want.

[Pause]

Loving and Forgiving Yourself

Loving yourself and forgiving and letting go of things you think you did wrong can be a huge issue for some people. It can stand in the way of emotional healing and balance.

Combine this meditation with the solfeggio frequency that relates to the heart chakra, which is 639 Hz. It promotes healing through love and brings about a profound connection to the self and others.

An alternative frequency to use is 741 Hz that relates to the throat chakra. It heals and balances the ability to speak one's truth with love and peace, and increases self-confidence.

Find a comfortable position, whether it is lying down or sitting.

If you are sitting, fold your hands loosely in your lap. Keep your feet next to each other on the floor.

If you prefer lying down, stretch your legs out straight and do not cross your ankles. Let your arms lie on the bed or fold your hands over your middle.

Place a pillow under your knees if that is more comfortable for you—your aim is loving yourself and allowing yourself space to be the glorious being you are.

Become aware of the surfaces touching you. Are they warm, soft, smooth, or coarse? Notice the support it is giving you and where your body feels the support the most.

Breathe in deeply and let the air fill your abdomen and your chest. Feel the air moving into your lungs and expand your chest.

Become aware of all the sensations in your chest. Do you feel any constriction? Do you feel open and receptive? Do you feel the need to close and protect?

Let the openness spread to your throat, connecting your throat with your chest cavity.

Breathe in...and out.

And in...and out.

And again, breathe in...and out.

And in...and out.

Feel the vastness inside you and know that is the true essence of the self you often hurt and judge. Know you have no beginning and no end and you are truly wonderful, worthy of love.

Know that you deserve to be loved and cared for and accepted. You are precious and unique.

Breathe in...and out.

And in...and out.

And again, breathe in...and out.

And in...and out.

Hold a warm feeling of acceptance and caring for yourself inside and allow it to expand and fill you with warmth as far as it will go. Do not force anything, just let it move.

[Pause]

Form an intention in your mind to forgive yourself for all the times you did not love yourself. To forgive yourself for all the things you think you did wrong or neglected to do.

Hold the loving, forgiving intention in your mind and give it a color and a form. Turn it around and look at it from all sides. Is it soft or hard? Is it round or square? Is it long or short? Is it a heart or any other recognizable shape?

Is it pulsating? Is it emitting light? Is it sparkling?

What is the color? Is it perhaps a warm pink or a deep, restful green? Or is it a calm blue? Perhaps an intense purple?

Breathe in...and out.

And in...and out.

And again, breathe in...and out.

And in...and out.

See the loving intention in the full form and color you imagine it, filling you with its love. Imagine it pushing out any unkindness and hate and filling every corner of your being with love and appreciation and forgiveness for yourself.

Become aware of how peaceful this makes you feel. Feel the wonderful stillness that has descended over you like a soft blanket, now the war inside is gone.

Savor the peace, warmth, and quiet.

Breathe in...and out.

And in...and out.

And again, breathe in...and out.

And in...and out.

[Pause]

When you are ready, say the following affirmations in your mind:

I forgive and love myself unconditionally and without boundaries.

I accept myself unconditionally and without reservations.

I care for myself, my health, and my inner peace because I know I deserve it.

I care for myself with joy and ease, it is not a burden.

I release any feelings of guilt and unworthiness because they no longer serve me.

Breathe in...and out.

And in...and out.

And again, breathe in...and out.

And in...and out.

Repeat your affirmations again, as many times as you want.

I forgive and love myself unconditionally and without boundaries.

I accept myself unconditionally and without reservations.

I care for myself, my health, and my inner peace because I know I deserve it.

I care for myself with joy and ease, it is not a burden.

I release any feelings of guilt and unworthiness because they no longer serve me.

Breathe in...and out.

And in...and out.

And again, breathe in...and out.

And in...and out.

I forgive and love myself unconditionally and without boundaries.

I accept myself unconditionally and without reservations.

I care for myself, my health, and my inner peace because I know I deserve it.

I care for myself with joy and ease, it is not a burden.

I release any feelings of guilt and unworthiness because they no longer serve me.

Breathe in...and out.

And in...and out.

And again, breathe in...and out.

And in...and out.

Move your awareness back to your chest and throat. Has anything changed? Do you breathe easier? Do you feel calmer and more relaxed?

Know that whenever in the future you find you're being unkind to yourself, you can come back to the loving intention you held earlier and let it spread its magic of warmth and love and forgiveness and acceptance again, to fill your being.

Releasing Trauma

Trauma can get embedded deep in our minds and bodies, causing diseases and mental problems. It can be buried so deep we might forget that it ever happened, but that will not heal the consequences of the trauma on our well-being.

Release conscious and subconsciously stored trauma with this guided meditation. Choose any nature sounds to play in the background while doing the script. It can be anything that calms and soothes you, such as a light breeze ruffling the leaves, or water flowing happily over pebbles.

It is not recommended choosing upbeat sounds such as a crackling campfire, even if you are particularly fond of the image. The flames are not restful and such images can heighten sensations of anxiety that might be brought forward when working with the traumatic memories.

Find a comfortable chair to sit on, lie down on a bed, or choose a couch that is long enough for you to stretch your legs out fully. Keep your arms by your sides and your hands flat when lying down, or comfortably fold your hands over your midriff. If you choose a sitting position, hold your hands relaxed and loose in your lap. Keep your legs and ankles uncrossed to help improve blood flow.

Close your eyes if you feel comfortable doing so. If it makes you feel anxious, fix your unfocused, soft gaze somewhere ahead or on the floor.

Know that you are safe and protected in this moment and you can relax.

Breathe this assurance in deeply, from your abdomen. Keep your shoulders down and relaxed, do not pull them up to breathe. Feel a warm, safe feeling spreading through your abdomen, chest, and throat, enveloping your heart in soft restfulness.

Exhale fully and visualize taking any tightness or discomfort out on the breath.

Breathe the assurance of safety in again, and exhale stress and fear.

Breathe in...and out.

And in...and out.

Take a moment to repeat to yourself, "I am safe. I am free."

And again..."I am safe. I am free."

Breathe in...and out.

And in...and out.

Feel any tight bands around your body loosening while you savor your affirmation as many times as you would like.

"I am safe. I am free."

And again..."I am safe. I am free."

Breathe in...and out.

And in...and out.

[Pause]

Now allow yourself to recall the memory of the trauma or as much of it as you can remember. Just let the picture flood your mind. Don't think rational thoughts about them, don't try to tell yourself what you should have done—just let the movie play in your mind.

Turn your awareness back to your body. Do you feel new sensations anywhere that were not there before your mind movie?

Acknowledge any feeling and physical sensation without trying to change them.

Repeat your affirmations and breathe.

"I am safe. I am free."

And again..."I am safe. I am free."

Breathe in...and out.

And in...and out.

"I am safe. I am free."

And again..."I am safe. I am free."

Breathe in...and out.

And in...and out.

[Pause]

Now check your body for any specific location where you feel the tension stronger than anywhere else. It could be an ache or a vague sense of discomfort. It could be a feeling of constriction or nausea.

Continue breathing deeply and calmly and visualize sending the breath like a golden light to the affected part of your body. Imagine the golden light flooding and bathing that part, loosening tightness and soothing pain.

If you feel emotions rising, let them and acknowledge them as voices from your higher self that have come to cleanse and free you. Let them wash over you while you breathe deeply and calmly.

Is there one emotion that stands out stronger than the others? Where do you feel this emotion?

Send the golden light of your breath to the muscles and organs where you experience the strong emotion.

Ask the muscles to become soft. Don't try to force anything, just ask them by repeating calmly, "Soft...soft...soft."

You are not trying to make the emotions or the hurt go away by asking them to soften, you are just asking them to soften around the discomfort.

"Soft...soft...soft."

Breathe in...and out.

And in...and out.

[Pause]

Savor the softness that has come and thank your muscles and organs for allowing the softness in.

Acknowledge that the hurt and the tension are still there but that it is softer around them.

Find peace in knowing that every time you ask them to soften a bit more, they will do so until they will no longer hold on to the hurting, traumatic memories. The memories will simply float away, exhaled on the golden light of your breath.

You are becoming whole once again and all is well.

"I am safe. I am free."

And again..."I am safe. I am free."

Breathe in...and out.

And in...and out.

Return your awareness to your surroundings when you feel ready. Stir your arms and legs slightly and open your eyes.

A Humming Meditation

Whether it is humming your favorite tune or sounding like a

bumblebee without a melody, humming is a powerful enhancer of intentions and images.

You can either do a humming meditation in the traditional way, keeping your hands relaxed, or you can put your thumbs in your ears with your fingers draped over your forehead. Closing your ears in this way will amplify the humming sound, making the vibrations even stronger.

The beauty in humming lies in the fact that regular daily activities don't need to be stopped if a quick vibrational reset is needed. You can hum softly under your breath while walking, driving, or doing anything where the sound won't disturb someone else.

For the following script, it is assumed that you are meditating only and keeping your hands relaxed. Adapt it in any way you would like.

Sit or lie down comfortably. Keep your legs straight, your feet together, and your ankles uncrossed.

Breathe in deeply from your abdomen, keeping your shoulders still.

Exhale fully.

Notice if you have any discomfort or pain anywhere in your body that you would like to send humming vibrations to.

Reflect on whether you're holding any intention for something you want to achieve or a sensation or perception you want to change. Formulate your intention in words to yourself, as clearly as you can.

Breathe in again...and out.

Breathe in...and let your breath out on a gentle hum. Don't force your voice and keep it soft. You can keep your lips closed or open them slightly, whatever feels natural and comfortable to you.

Breathe in...and out on mmm...

And breathe in...and out on mmm.

Breathe in...and out on mmm...

And breathe in...and out on mmm.

Become aware of where in your body you feel the vibrations of the humming. Are they in your head, your heart, your throat, or your stomach? Are the vibrations awakening any other sensations in your body?

Keep humming softly for as long as you want, noticing the vibrations move through you.

Breathe in...and out on mmm...

And breathe in...and out on mmm.

Breathe in...and out on mmm...

And breathe in...and out on mmm.

[Pause]

Now, direct the vibrations to the body part that you want to heal or relax. Picture the vibrations as a golden spiral that gently turns, rubbing, and brushing that body part with calmness, softness, and health.

Breathe in...and breathe the golden spiral out on mmm...

And breathe in...and out on mmm.

Breathe in...and breathe the golden spiral out on mmm...

And breathe in...and out on mmm.

Turn your mind back to the intention you formulated earlier. Visualize the words of the intention tangling with the golden spiral, becoming one with it. Imagine the intention being carried with the spiral to every fiber of your being.

Keep doing it for as long as you want.

Breathe in...and breathe the golden spiral out on mmm...

And breathe in...and out on mmm.

Breathe in...and breathe the golden spiral out on mmm...

And breathe in...and out on mmm.

[Pause]

When you feel ready, stop exhaling the golden spiral and the hum. Breathe normally but deeply for as long as it takes to return your awareness to your surroundings.

Breathe in again...and out.

[Pause]

Gently open your eyes.

CONCLUSION

I sincerely wish that the journey through sound healing you took with me in this book has changed your life for the better in profound ways.

Take what you have learned with you on the road to becoming the best version of yourself you can be, as you were intended to become from the beginning of time.

You are now equipped with an understanding of how important and fundamental all sound is for life. You understand how sound shaped us and continues to mold us—it is up to us to use it wisely.

You have also learned how to adapt sound to make your life easier, calmer, and hopefully, less painful.

You have, indeed, accomplished an act of creation. Well done!

May you travel forward with love, light, and courage.

CONSIDER A REVIEW

You have taken the first step to a life beyond your wildest imagination, by reading this book and implementing the techniques to balance and heal your mental, physical, and emotional body.

Open the way for others to find the information too, by leaving a positive review.

May your sound journey truly be blessed.

REFERENCES

Abhang, P. A., Gawali, B. W., & Mehrotra, S. C. (2016). *Introduction to EEG- and speech-based emotion recognition*. Amsterdam Elsevier. https://www.elsevier.com/books/introduction-to-eeg-and-speech-based-emotion-recognition/abhang/978-0-12-804490-2

Aller, M., Giani, A., Conrad, V., Watanabe, M., & Noppeney, U. (2015). A spatially collocated sound thrusts a flash into awareness. *Frontiers in Integrative Neuroscience*, 9. https://doi.org/10.3389/fnint.2015.00016

Ankrom, S. (2019). *How to breathe properly for relieving your anxiety*. Verywell Mind. https://www.verywellmind.com/abdominal-breathing-2584115

Atkins, S. (2015, August 21). *A beginner's guide to essential Sanskrit mantras*. Sonima. https://www.sonima.com/yoga/sanskrit-mantras/

Bakken Center for Spirituality and Healing. (2015, October 19). *Deep listening*. Center for Spirituality and Healing - University of Minnesota. https://www.csh.umn.edu/education/focus-areas/whole-systems-healing/leadership/deep-listening#:~:text=Deep%20listening%20is%20a%20process

Balezin, M., Baryshnikova, K. V., Kapitanova, P., & Evlyukhin, A. B. (2018). Electromagnetic properties of the Great Pyramid: First multipole resonances and energy concentration. *Journal of Applied Physics*, *124*(3), 034903. https://doi.org/10.1063/1.5026556

Balsamo, G., & Dagnese, L. F. (2012). *The Book of Breathing*. Robin.
Basner, M., Clark, C., Hansell, A., Hileman, J. I., Janssen, S., Shepherd, K., & Sparrow, V. (2017). Aviation noise impacts: State of the science. *Noise & Health*, *19*(87), 41–50. https://doi.org/10.4103/nah.NAH_104_16

Berkovich–Ohana, A., Wilf, M., Kahana, R., Arieli, A., & Malach, R. (2015). Repetitive speech elicits widespread deactivation in the human cortex: The "mantra" effect?. *Brain and Behavior*, *5*(7). https://doi.org/10.1002/brb3.346

Bhaumik, G. (2019, December 27). *Sound healing explained - how it works and health benefits*. Destination Deluxe. https://destinationdeluxe.com/sound-healing-health-benefits/

Biblioteka Records. (2015, October). *The solfeggio frequencies*. BIBLIOTEKA RECORDS. https://www.biblioteka.world/our-blog/2020/9/27/the-solfeggio-frequencies#:~:text=The%20Solfeggio%20Frequencies%3A%20Where%20Did%20They%20Come%20From%3F&text=In%20the%2011th%20century%2C%20a

Boccia, M., Piccardi, L., & Guariglia, P. (2015). The meditative mind: A comprehensive meta-analysis of MRI studies. *BioMed Research International*, *2015*, 1–11. https://doi.org/10.1155/2015/419808

Booth, S. (2018, June 10). *Brain health with binaural beats*. Healthline. https://www.healthline.com/health-news/your-brain-on-binaural-beats#The-illusion-of-binaural-beats

Buddha Groove. (n.d.). *Traditional Tibetan tingsha cymbals / Meaning and origins*. Www.buddhagroove.com. https://www.buddhagroove.com/buddhist-ritual-tool-tingsha/

Chaieb, L., Wilpert, E. C., Reber, T. P., & Fell, J. (2015). Auditory beat stimulation and its effects on cognition and mood states. *Frontiers in Psychiatry*, *6*. https://doi.org/10.3389/fpsyt.2015.00070

Chepesiuk, R. (2005). Decibel hell: The effects of living in a noisy world. *Environmental Health Perspectives*, *113*(1). https://doi.org/10.1289/ehp.113-a434

Clason, D. (2019, September 16). *Tinnitus sound therapy - how it works*. Healthy Hearing. https://www.healthyhearing.com/report/52999-Tinnitus-sound-therapy-retraining-the-way-the-brain-perceives-sound

Cooper, B. B. (2013, August 21). *What is meditation & how does it affect our brains?* Buffer Resources. https://buffer.com/resources/how-meditation-affects-your-brain/

Cymascope. (n.d.). *Home of the cymatics*. Cymascope. Retrieved 2021, from https://www.cymascope.com/cyma_research/egyptology.html

Dargie, D. (1991). Umngqokolo: Xhosa overtone singing and the song Nondel'ekhaya. *African Music: Journal of the International Library of African Music*, *7*(1), 33–47. https://doi.org/10.21504/amj.v7i1.1928

Davisi, J. (2021, March 2). *10-Minute meditation for depression*. Www.youtube.com. https://www.youtube.com/watch?v=xRxT9cOKiM8

Deva, C. (2018, June 19). *Emotional and mental causes of illness. The list by Louise Hay*. Heartland Healing Arts. https://www.heartlandhealingarts. com/blog/2018/6/19/emotional-and-mental-causes-of-illness-the-list-by-louise-hay

Encyclopedia.com. (2014). *Sound therapy*. Encyclopedia.com. https:// www.encyclopedia.com/medicine/encyclopedias-almanacs-transcripts-and-maps/sound-therapy

Erkkilä, J., Punkanen, M., Fachner, J., Ala-Ruona, E., Pöntiö, I., Tervaniemi, M., Vanhala, M., & Gold, C. (2011). Individual music therapy for depression: Randomised controlled trial. *British Journal of Psychiatry, 199*(2), 132–139. https://doi.org/10.1192/bjp.bp.110.085431

Estrada, J. (2020, March 25). *3 ways to bring your body vibrational balance using sound healing therapy*. Well+Good. https://www.wellandgood.com/sound-healing/

European Environment Agency. (n.d.). *Noise*. European Environment Agency. https://www.eea.europa.eu/themes/human/noise

Fellows, E. (n.d.). *Traveling the energetic highway: What are meridians?* Www.centerpointhealing.com. https://www.centerpointhealing.com/hyattsville/traveling-the-energetic-highway-what-are-meridians/#:~:text=The%20simplest%20definition%20is%20that

Feuerstein, G. (2011). *The deeper dimension of yoga: Theory and practice*. Shambhala.

Finne, P., & Petersen, T. H. (n.d.). *Traffic noise is dangerous to our health – but what do we do about it?* Forcetechnology.com. https://forcetechnology.com/en/articles/traffic-noise-dangerous-health-what-to-do-about-it

Flood, L. (2016, September 16). *Qi gong's healing sounds practice*. Chopra. https://chopra.com/articles/qi-gongs-healing-sounds-practice

Gabriel, R. (2015, January 15). *How to Use Sound to Heal Yourself*. Chopra. https://chopra.com/articles/how-to-use-sound-to-heal-yourself

Gadberry, A. L. (2011). Steady beat and state anxiety. *Journal of Music Therapy, 48*(3), 346–356. https://doi.org/10.1093/jmt/48.3.346

Gingras, B., Pohler, G., & Fitch, W. T. (2014). Exploring shamanic journeying: Repetitive drumming with shamanic instructions induces specific subjective experiences but no larger cortisol decrease than instrumental meditation music. *PLoS ONE, 9*(7), e102103. https://doi.org/10.1371/journal.pone.0102103

Goldman, J. (1996). *Healing sounds: The power of harmonics*. Element Books.

Goldman, J. (2009a). The basic principle of sound healing. *Jonathan Goldman's Healing Sounds*. https://www.healingsounds.com/the-basic-principle-of-sound-healing/#:~:text=A%20concept%20of%20using%20sound,of%20using%20sound%20to%20heal.

Goldman, J. (2009b, March 25). *Everything is in a state of vibration*. Www.youtube.com. https://www.youtube.com/watch?v=gHb3ZyıQgyQ

Hanlon, B. (n.d.). *9 solfeggio frequencies*. Bríd Hanlon. https://www.bridhanlon.com/healy-therapist-programs/nine-solfeggio-frequencies

Hatton, J. (2018). What are the dangers or side effects of binaural beats? [YouTube Video]. In *YouTube*. https://www.youtube.com/watch?v=aXi_hIdovpU

Hunt, J. (2020, May 28). *What is primordial sound meditation? The four soul questions | Personal mantra | Four intentions.* Www.youtube.com. https://www.youtube.com/watch?v=URwQoFvk9Qo

Inner Health Studio. (2012). *Relaxation for pain management: Free relaxation script.* Www.innerhealthstudio.com. https://www.innerhealthstudio.com/pain-management.html

Inner Health Studio. (2020). *Generalized anxiety relaxation: Free relaxation script.* Www.innerhealthstudio.com. https://www.innerhealthstudio.com/generalized-anxiety-relaxation.html

Isahak, D. A. F. (2005, March 27). *Five-elements qigong.* The Star. https://www.thestar.com.my/lifestyle/health/2005/03/27/fiveelements-qigong#:~:text=Today%20I%20will%20share%20with

Kaku, Dr. M. (2011). The universe is a symphony of vibrating strings [YouTube Video]. In *YouTube.* https://www.youtube.com/watch?v=fW6JFKgbAF4

Kappert, M. B., Wuttke-Linnemann, A., Schlotz, W., & Nater, U. M. (2019). The aim justifies the means—differences among musical and nonmusical means of relaxation or activation induction in daily life. *Frontiers in Human Neuroscience, 13.* https://doi.org/10.3389/fnhum.2019.00036

Kučera, O., & Havelka, D. (2012). Mechano-electrical vibrations of microtubules—link to subcellular morphology. *BioSystems, 109*(3), 346–355. https://doi.org/10.1016/j.biosystems.2012.04.009

Lazzerini, E. (2019, June 15). *How to cleanse crystals with a singing bowl.* Ethan Lazzerini. https://www.ethanlazzerini.com/cleanse-crystals-with-a-singing-bowl/

Lin, K. (n.d.). *Arthur Sullivan – The lost chord*. Genius.com. https://genius.com/Arthur-sullivan-the-lost-chord-lyrics

Lochte, B. C., Guillory, S. A., Richard, C. A. H., & Kelley, W. M. (2018). An fMRI investigation of the neural correlates underlying the autonomous sensory meridian response (ASMR). *BioImpacts, 8*(4), 295–304. https://doi.org/10.15171/bi.2018.32

MacMillan, A. (2017, April 5). *Why nature sounds help you relax, according to science*. Health.com. https://www.health.com/condition/stress/why-nature-sounds-are-relaxing

Marsab Music Management. (n.d.). *Cuncordu e tenore de Orosei*. Marsab. http://www.marsab.net/tenores-2/

Mauli. (n.d.). *What are the 5 elements in Ayurveda?* Mauli Rituals. https://www.maulirituals.com/blogs/news/what-are-the-5-elements-in-ayurveda

McCraty, R., Atkinson, M., Tiller, W. A., Rein, G., & Watkins, A. D. (1995). The effects of emotions on short-term power spectrum analysis of heart rate variability. *The American Journal of Cardiology, 76*(14), 1089–1093. https://doi.org/10.1016/s0002-9149(99)80309-9

Mehta, R., Zhu, R. (Juliet), & Cheema, A. (2012). Is noise always bad? Exploring the effects of ambient noise on creative cognition. *Journal of Consumer Research, 39*(4), 784–799. https://doi.org/10.1086/665048

Mind Tools Content Team. (2012). *Physical relaxation techniques: Deep breathing, PMR, and centering*. Mindtools.com. https://www.mindtools.com/pages/article/newTCS_05.htm

Miranda, Dr. R. A. (2020, February 22). *Do binaural beats work?* Www.youtube.com. https://www.youtube.com/watch?v=Om3zB35xxTo

Mogg, K., Bradley, B. P., Williams, R., & Mathews, A. (1993). Subliminal processing of emotional information in anxiety and depression. *Journal of Abnormal Psychology, 102*(2), 304–311. https://doi.org/10.1037/0021-843x.102.2.304

Molesworth, BrettR. C., Burgess, M., & Gunnell, B. (2013). Using the effect of alcohol as a comparison to illustrate the detrimental effects of noise on performance. *Noise and Health, 15*(66), 367. https://doi.org/10.4103/1463-1741.116565

Moss, A. S., Wintering, N., Roggenkamp, H., Khalsa, D. S., Waldman, M. R., Monti, D., & Newberg, A. B. (2012). Effects of an 8-week meditation program on mood and anxiety in patients with memory loss. *The Journal of Alternative and Complementary Medicine, 18*(1), 48–53. https://doi.org/10.1089/acm.2011.0051

National Center for Environmental Health. (2019, October 7). *What noises cause hearing loss?* Centers for Disease Control and Prevention. https://www.cdc.gov/nceh/hearing_loss/what_noises_cause_hearing_loss.html

National Geographic Society. (2019, July 16). *Noise Pollution.* National Geographic Society. https://www.nationalgeographic.org/encyclopedia/noise-pollution/

National Institute on Deafness and Other Communication Disorders, Maryland. (2015, August 18). *How do we hear?* NIDCD. https://www.nidcd.nih.gov/health/how-do-we-hear#:~:text=Sound%20waves%20enter%20the%20outer

O'Brien, T. (2019, December 8). *Six healing sounds (simple) for anxiety depression.* Www.youtube.com. https://www.youtube.com/watch?v=i8UovBIlM1o

Omnivos Therapeutics. (n.d.). *Education*. Www.omnivos.com. https:// www.omnivos.com/education

Prestwood, K. M. (2003). Energy medicine: What is it, how does it work, and what place does it have in orthopedics? *Techniques in Orthopaedics*, *18*(1), 46–53. https://doi.org/10.1097/00013611- 200303000-00009

Price, S. (2021, April 13). *Cymatics for healthcare: Applying the science of sound in cancer surgery*. Health Europa. https://www.healtheuropa.eu/ cymatics-for-healthcare-applying-the-science-of-sound-in-cancer- surgery/107471/

Pujol, S., Berthillier, M., Defrance, J., Lardies, J., Levain, J.-P. ., Petit, R., Houot, H., & Mauny, F. (2014). Indoor noise exposure at home: A field study in the family of urban schoolchildren. *Indoor Air*, *24*(5), 511– 520. https://doi.org/10.1111/ina.12094

Rivera-Dugenio, J. (2019). The language of our DNA-scalar energy. In *International Journal of Advanced Research and Publications*. http://www. ijarp.org/published-research-papers/mar2019/The-Language-Of-Our- Dna-Scalar-Energy.pdf

Rodrigues, S. (2020, May). *Conscious listening and sound perception*. Explore Life. https://www.explore-life.com/en/articles/conscious- listening-and-sound-perception

Root-Bernstein, M., & Root-Bernstein, R. (2010). *Einstein On creative thinking: Music and the intuitive art of scientific imagination*. Psychology Today. https://www.psychologytoday.com/us/blog/imagine/201003/ einstein-creative-thinking-music-and-the-intuitive-art-scientific- imagination

Rubik, B., Muehsam, D., Hammerschlag, R., & Jain, S. (2015). Biofield science and healing: History, terminology, and concepts. *Global*

Advances in Health and Medicine, 4(1_suppl), gahmj.2015.038. https://doi. org/10.7453/gahmj.2015.038.suppl

Russo, M. A., Santarelli, D. M., & O'Rourke, D. (2017). The physiological effects of slow breathing in the healthy human. *Breathe*, *13*(4), 298–309. https://doi.org/10.1183/20734735.009817

Santos-Longhurst, A. (2020, January 27). *Music as therapy: The uses and benefits of sound healing.* Healthline; Healthline Media. https://www. healthline.com/health/sound-healing#types

Satchwell, J. (2019, October 15). *3 ways to reduce pain with tuning forks.* Www.academyofsoundhealing.com. https://www. academyofsoundhealing.com/blog/3-ways-tuning-forks-can-reduce-pain

Scialla, J. (2019). *History of crystals and healing.* Crystalage.com. https:// www.crystalage.com/crystal_information/crystal_history/

Scott, E. (2020a, June 29). *How noise pollution might be increasing your stress levels.* Verywell Mind. https://www.verywellmind.com/stress-and-noise-pollution-how-you-may-be-at-risk-3145041

Scott, E. (2020b, November 30). *Why noise is truly stressful and what to do about it.* Verywell Mind. https://www.verywellmind.com/how-to-reduce-noise-pollutions-negative-effects-3144733

Scott, E. (2021, January 5). *What You Need to Know About the Stress Hormone.* Verywell Mind. https://www.verywellmind.com/cortisol-and-stress-how-to-stay-healthy-3145080

Shanti Bowl. (n.d.). *How singing bowls work: The science of singing bowls.* Shanti Bowl. https://www.shantibowl.com/blogs/blog/how-singing-bowls-work-the-science-behind-singing-bowls

Shanti Bowl. (2021). *How to choose a singing bowl: Complete guide (Updated 2021)*. Shanti Bowl. https://www.shantibowl.com/blogs/blog/how-to-choose-a-singing-bowl

Smithsonian. (n.d.). *Smithsonian - tuning forks*. Americanhistory.si.edu. https://americanhistory.si.edu/science/tuningfork.htm

Snow, S. (2011). *Healing through sound: An exploration of a vocal sound healing method in Great Britain* [Thesis]. https://spectrum.library.concordia.ca/7351/1/Snow_PhD_S2011.pdf

Socratic. (2016, February 21). *What is the difference between an overtone and a harmonic?* Socratic.org. https://socratic.org/questions/what-is-the-difference-between-an-overtone-and-a-harmonic

Sørensen, M., Andersen, Z. J., Nordsborg, R. B., Becker, T., Tjønneland, A., Overvad, K., & Raaschou-Nielsen, O. (2013). Long-term exposure to road traffic noise and incident diabetes: A cohort study. *Environmental Health Perspectives*, *121*(2), 217–222. https://doi.org/10.1289/ehp.1205503

Sound Coherence. (n.d.). *Tom Hunt*. Www.soundcoherence.com. http://www.soundcoherence.com/about

Stelter, G. (2016, December 18). *A beginner's guide to the 7 chakras and their meanings*. Healthline; Healthline Media. https://www.healthline.com/health/fitness-exercise/7-chakras

Tenpenny, K. (2016, April 12). *Vocal toning- vowel sounds of each chakra and soul*. Www.youtube.com. https://www.youtube.com/watch?v=e5vbOpl6zS4

The Light of Happiness. (2021a, July 9). *9 best Tibetan singing bowls, plus 1 to avoid (2021 buyers guide) | The Light Of Happiness*. The Light of Happiness. https://www.thelightofhappiness.com/best-singing-bowls/

The Light of Happiness. (2021b, July 9). *9 best tuning forks for healing, plus 1 to avoid (2021 buyers guide)*. The Light of Happiness. https://www. thelightofhappiness.com/best-tuning-forks-for-healing/

The Meditation Trust. (n.d.). *How is transcendental meditation different?* The Meditation Trust. https://www.meditationtrust.com/how-is-transcendental-meditation-different/

The Physics Classroom. (n.d.). *Physics tutorial: Resonance*. Www.physicsclassroom.com. https://www.physicsclassroom.com/Class/sound/U11l5a.cfm#:~:text=This%20is%20known%20as%20resonance

Thorp, T. (2021, January 14). *The Chopra Center*. The Chopra Center. https://chopra.com/articles/what-is-a-mantra

TMHome. (n.d.). *Origins - Where does transcendental meditation come from?* Transcendental Meditation: LATEST NEWS & OPINIONS. https://tmhome.com/why-should-i-take-up-transcendental-meditation/origins/

Tools for Wellness. (n.d.). *Fibonacci tuning fork set*. Tools for Wellness. https://www.toolsforwellness.com/product/fibonacci-tuning-fork-set/

Traditional Chinese Medicine World Foundation. (2019). *Meridian connection*. TCM World; https://www.tcmworld.org/what-is-tcm/meridian-connection/

Treasure, J. (2013). *Conscious listening*. Www.imdrt.org. http://www.imdrt.org/mentoring

Treasure, J. (2017). *How to be heard: Secrets for powerful speaking and listening*. Coral Gables, Fl Mango Publishing Group.

Treasure, J. (2020, September 18). *Transform your relationships with three types of listening*. Www.juliantreasure.com. https://www.juliantreasure.

com/blog/types-listening-relationships#:~:text=Outer%20listening%
20is%20the%20process

Trice, E. (2020, August 15). *Buying my own singing bowl transformed my meditation practice.* Shape. https://www.shape.com/lifestyle/mind-and-body/tibetan-singing-bowl-meditation

University Of Maryland Medical Center. (2005, March 16). *Laughter helps blood vessels function better.* ScienceDaily. https://www.sciencedaily.com/releases/2005/03/050310100458.htm

University of Toronto Computer Science. (2004). *What Is Sound?* http://www.cs.toronto.edu/~gpenn/csc401/soundASR.pdf

Voigt, J. (2012). *The six healing sounds: Chinese mantras for purifying the body, mind, and soul.* Www.qi-Journal.com. https://www.qi-journal.com/qigong-meditation/qigong-ch-i-kung/2809-six-healing-sounds

Voigt, J. (2013). *The man who invented "qigong."* Www.qigonginstitute.org. https://www.qigonginstitute.org

Wakeling, N. (2007, January 3). *Chakra toning.* Sound Intentions. https://www.soundintentions.com/sound-healing/exercises/chakra-toning/

Walsh, K. M., Saab, B. J., & Farb, N. A. (2019). Effects of a mindfulness meditation app on subjective well-being: Active randomized controlled trial and experience sampling study. *JMIR Mental Health, 6*(1), e10844. https://doi.org/10.2196/10844

Wang, H., Tang, D., Wu, Y., Zhou, L., & Sun, S. (2020). The state of the art of sound therapy for subjective tinnitus in adults. *Therapeutic Advances in Chronic Disease, 11,* 204062232095642. https://doi.org/10.1177/2040622320956426

Weller, L. (2020, September 3). *How the chakra system relates to the solfeggio scale*. Binaural Beats Freak. https://www.binauralbeatsfreak. com/sound-therapy/solfeggio-frequencies-chakra-system

WHO. (2021, April 13). *Noncommunicable diseases*. Who.int; World Health Organization: WHO. https://www.who.int/news-room/fact-sheets/detail/noncommunicable-diseases

Wired. (2019). A neuroscientist explains ASMR's effects on the brain & the body. In *YouTube*. https://www.youtube.com/watch? v=IiuUfX2cbhU

Yogapedia. (2017, January 8). *Yoga dictionary*. Www.yogapedia.com. https://www.yogapedia.com/definition

Yugay, I. (2019, January 10). *Everything you need to know about sound healing*. Mindvalley Blog. https://blog.mindvalley.com/sound-healing/? epik=djoyJnU9eFhxMTdqTFR2c2dSRUVCQXQ4Q1hNLTRJQkdL b19HeWkmcDowJm49NiiISotrVWUxOUxzc3QyWDFGbGVDdyZ oPUFBQUFBR0VINmxr

Zevitas, C. D., Spengler, J. D., Jones, B., McNeely, E., Coull, B., Cao, X., Loo, S. M., Hard, A.-K., & Allen, J. G. (2018). Assessment of noise in the airplane cabin environment. *Journal of Exposure Science & Environmental Epidemiology*, *28*(6), 568–578. https://doi.org/10.1038/s41370-018-0027-z

Images

3centista. (2020). A traditional djembe. In *Pixabay*. https://pixabay.com/photos/djemba-africa-instrument-music-4931869/

Altmann, G. (2012). The right frequency is life. In *Pixabay*. https://pixabay.com/illustrations/heart-curve-health-pulse-frequency-66888/

AniaPM. (2021a). A rainstick. In *Pixabay*. https://pixabay.com/photos/rain-stick-music-instrument-6117677/

AniaPM. (2021b). Kalimbas range from fairly sophisticated to very basic. In *Pixabay*. https://pixabay.com/photos/music-kalimba-instrument-6117640/

Auntmasako. (2016). A set of tuning forks. In *Pixabay*. https://pixabay.com/photos/tuning-fork-healing-brain-tuner-1902632/

Bartfai, L. (2018). Crystal singing bowls. In *Pixabay*. https://pixabay.com/photos/sound-sound-health-meditation-3521140/

Braxmeier, H. (2011). A set of gongs, with singing bowls in the foreground. In *Pixabay*. https://pixabay.com/photos/gong-mark-up-idiot-self-tönendes-11484/

Ebrahimnia, F. (2021). Hanghang can vary from small to large. In *Pixabay*. https://pixabay.com/photos/hang-drum-music-musician-5684668/

Firmbee. (2015). Solfeggio and earphones. In *Pixabay*. https://pixabay.com/photos/mobile-phone-iphone-music-616012/

Free-Photos. (2015). City noise does not even stop at night. In *Pixabay*. https://pixabay.com/photos/city-people-street-traffic-night-690158/

Lindl, C. (2019). Several monochords sharing a single sound box to demonstrate harmonic intervals. In *Pixabay*. https://pixabay.com/photos/body-monochord-monochord-haselholz-4352645/

Lolé, O. (2019). A hammered dulcimer. In *Pixabay*. https://pixabay.com/photos/hammered-dulcimer-instrument-strings-4481476/

Perry, J. R. (2014). A modern street musician playing a large didgeridoo. In *Pixabay*. https://pixabay.com/photos/didgeridoo-street-music-man-people-446132/

Photos. (2013). A traditional musician holding a native American flute. In *Pixabay*. https://pixabay.com/photos/native-american-courting-flute-176096/

Rickhuss, S. (2018). Gemstones used in natural healing. In *Pixabay*. https://pixabay.com/photos/natural-healing-gemstones-blue-bag-3371814/

Segado, J. F. (2015). Traditional Buddhist tingshas. In *Pixabay*. https://pixabay.com/photos/tingshas-buddhism-meditation-peace-1041584/

Sundermeier, A. (2019). Earplugs are not always the best solution. In *Pixabay*. https://pixabay.com/photos/ear-plug-noise-protection-4085688/

Time Traveler Al. (2020). Quartz rock crystal. In *Pixabay*. https://pixabay.com/photos/crystal-quartz-rock-crystal-5025318/

Wolter, T. (2019). Hearing is automatic but listening is not. In *Pixabay*. https://pixabay.com/photos/ear-mouth-nose-face-head-voices-3971050/

Zimmer, M. A. (2013). Singing bowls. In *Pixabay*. https://pixabay.com/photos/singing-bowl-singing-bowls-235266/

PLEASE LEAVE A REVIEW ON AMAZON

From the bottom of our hearts, thank you for reading this book. We truly hope that it helps you on your spiritual journey and to live a more empowered and happy life. Would you be kind enough to leave an honest review for this book on Amazon? We would be ecstatic to hear your feedback. Thank you and good luck,

Ascending Vibrations

JOIN OUR COMMUNITY

Why not join our Facebook community and discuss your spiritual path with like-minded seekers?

We would love to hear from you.

Go to this link to join the 'Ascending Vibrations' community: bit.ly/ascendingvibrations